SECUR
SALES LEADERSHIP

Practical & Proven Techniques That Will Unlock Your Teams Potential

Russ Ackerman

Published by
PSS Publishing
4331 Julington Creek Rd.
Jacksonville, Fl. 32258

rackerman@provensalesstrategies.com

For permission contact Russ Ackerman at:
Limit of Liability and Disclaimer of Warranty: The author has done his/her best to present accurate and up-to-date information in this book, but he/she cannot guarantee that the information is correct or will suit your particular situation, and the information provided herein is provided "as is.

Editor: Chuck Day, Jr.
SearchWrite Inc.
chuckday@bellsouth.net

Cover Designer: Dana Bussiere

Layout: DocUmeant Designs
www.DocUmeantDesigns.com

ISBN: 978-1974129010

Dedication

THIS BOOK IS dedicated to my wife Judy. She has been my partner and encourager for over 50 years. She has been a wonderful wife, an awesome mother and grandmother, and is highly respected by those that know her well. Her organizational skills have kept me on track amid the whirlwind of activity that has always been a part of our lives.

I would also like to include the men in my inner circle that have encouraged me to write this book. Each of these men are tops in their own fields and it has been my pleasure to meet with them individually, at least once a month or so, for the past few years. They are: Joe Hassan, Co-founder of Certified Security; Dave Strathmann, Crestcom International Bullet Proof Management; Jeremy Salem, President of Smart Step Media; Greg Gutkowski, best-selling author; Christian Abrahamson, President at Exigo Sales Consulting.

In addition, I would like to say thank you to the Honeywell organization for giving me the opportunities to speak and including me in their annual conventions and workshops throughout the years.

CONTENTS

Introduction

NOTHING HAPPENS UNTIL somebody sells something" is about as old a business axiom as has ever been written or proclaimed. But it is still as true as ever, a pillar of capitalism if there was one.

I know because I'm living proof of this axiom. I've been selling for more than 30 years, specifically both residential and commercial security systems. Selling has brought me more success and satisfaction than I ever imagined, and helped me build more friendships than I can ever count.

What I continue to sell today has far more benefits and capabilities than what I was selling a few years ago. But that only affirms the axiom. After all, somebody kept selling the ideas and the values of new features and benefits to decision-makers at Honeywell, ADT and numerous other companies. And everyone is better off for it.

I believe strongly that you will be better off reading and taking to heart what I'm sharing in the pages that follow.

My upmost desire here is to help. As I travel throughout the country consulting companies on my VIP days, I see so many sales managers and young sales people who have not had the advantages that I have had first-hand. These men and women have the potential to really make an impact and develop great careers for themselves and for others. My greatest reward is to have a small part in the success of someone else.

All that appears in these pages was written with the alarm and security systems industry in mind. It's the field I know best. But I believe what I am about to share also applies to many other industries. When push comes to shove, selling is still selling. It's a process—maybe even an art—that is critical to any business. As renowned management consultant Peter Drucker once observed, "The fact is, everybody—vice presidents, operations managers, HR directors, IT professionals, customer service representatives, accounting professionals, receptionists—can stay at home until somebody makes a sale."

I believe selling is something almost anyone can learn, and then master.

Not that it's easy. Far from it. Selling takes ambition, confidence, determination, inexhaustible discipline, an ocean of patience, a fierce will to win, and the ability to shrug off hearing "No, thanks" and "Go away! *ad nauseam.* Most important, selling demands a willingness to work hard and put in the time required. But the rewards of selling make it all worthwhile, as I am about to explain.

Now it's time for me to sell something: my ideas, suggestions, and the value of the lessons I've learned. That's so you can sell something, and sell it better and more successfully than you thought possible.

Russ Ackerman
Jacksonville, Florida
Summer 2017

Part I
Sales Leadership

THIS BOOK IS *written in two parts. This first section relates to the responsibilities of the sales leader and goes into great detail on how to accomplish the various duties that come with the title of Sales Manager. You have likely already read books on leadership, but the first part of this book is a practical, proven explanation of techniques that I have found to work when leading sales teams both large and small.*

In part #2, I include practical information for sharpening your sales skills.

CHAPTER 1

Congratulations! You're a Sales Manager. Now What?

Most people become managers just like they became parents. They wake up one day and they are one.

I COULDN'T BEGIN to tell you how many times I've posed this question throughout my career:

"What is the sales manager's most important responsibility?"

Most of the managers I posed this question to didn't have a clue. It startled me when I first discovered that sad truth, and startles me to this day. Worse, some of the clueless managers further admitted they hadn't ever given much thought to what their most important responsibility might be! Then again, many managers don't even have a job description. This simply blows me away.

> Too often the branch manager or owner will simply bestow the title of sales manager on the sales team's top producer.

SIMPLE
fact

How can you even begin building a sales team if you do not first have a solid understanding of the key requirements of your own job? Every sales manager—like every sales consultant—should have a *written* job description. If you don't have one, start writing, right now.

I'll give you a leg up by explaining what a professional sales manager's (i.e. *sales leader's*) job is really all about, and the responsibilities it includes. First, though, an observation: I have seen many individuals handed the sales manager's job who had no business holding that job. Too often the branch manager or owner will simply bestow the title of sales manager on the sales team's top producer. It's a knee-jerk decision that is usually a huge mistake. In many cases—if not most—the top producer on the sales team is not a team player and lacks the leadership skills to build a team. Yes, top-performing sales people usually are very competitive and, yes, they usually do score high on autonomy. That's fine; both traits are ones a champion sales representative needs to have. But they're NOT the traits that are essential to building and maintaining a productive sales team. It's a critical distinction. Indeed, it may be why many of football's most successful coaches and major league baseball managers were not stellar players.

SIMPLE *fact* | It is OK to sell the dream; just don't sell the job. | My own career is a good example. After working at Scott Alarm Systems for just a few months, I was given the responsibility and title of sales manager. I am sure I was given the job solely because I was generating so many sales that the owner concluded I should be able to train other people to follow in my footsteps. My owner concluded wrong. I wasn't much of a sales manager back then. In fact, I was pretty lousy. I did not have the skills sets required to handle the diverse responsibilities of the position. Recalling that stretch of my career is downright embarrassing, given some of the decision I made. Had I had this book back then, I know I would have been far more successful.

The sales leadership job is not for the weak. A sales manager routinely has to make difficult decisions when holding team members accountable. The position also requires creative ideas, a tremendously positive attitude that can withstand myriad challenges, plus a solid understanding—and embracing—of an axiom: The success of the sale office is largely his or her responsibility. In short, the job of the sales manager is strikingly different from that of the sales representative. Let's take a detailed look.

RECRUIT, INTERVIEW, AND HIRE

Years ago, I was enjoying a lunch with my mentor, the late Bill Kuchon. Bill was also a good friend and, in my opinion, the very finest sales and leadership trainer in the alarm industry. Spending time with Bill was always a learning experience, and on this day he asked me the same question I used to begin this chapter: *"What is a sales manager's most important responsibility?"* In truth, it was a loaded question, as I would come to realize.

"The number one job of a sales manager is to motivate the sales team I quickly replied," Bill immediately smiled, then told me my answer was wrong. Yes, he allowed, motivating is an important responsibility, but not the most important. What was job 1? "To build a sales team," Bill said with authority.

At the time I disagreed. But after years of working with sales teams large, small and in between, I've come to see the wisdom of the Bill's reasoning. The most important responsibility of any sales manager is, as Bill stated, to **build a sales team**. After all, if you don't have a team, there's no one to motivate. In building your sales team, here are a few fundamentals to keep in mind:

1. **Talent draws talent**—Set your standards high and demand excellence of your existing team. Hire only the best and you will soon find that other professional sales people will want to be part of your team.

2. **Hire for attitude**—I highly recommend reading Mark Murphy's book, "Hire for Attitude." It is the best book I have found on hiring, and fits the alarm industry to a tee.

3. **Plan ahead**—Always be looking for talented sales champions.

4. **Tolerate turnover**—Don't be discouraged when you lose your top producer. It's a fact of business life. Your best sales people are in the field every day and meeting numerous business owners, many of whom would love to have your best sales reps on their teams.

There now are more job-search sites on the internet than you can count. Ask other companies in your area which ones tend to attract the best candidates. When placing an ad on line, there are a few things that you must include. Post not only the approximate income potential, but also all of the company benefits. If you pay your reps straight commission, you need to brag about all the exciting benefits your company has to offer, such as 401(k) program. With employer-provided training itself now considered to be a big deal in the recruiting world, be sure to list that in your ad, too, if your company offers it.

When a candidate responds to your post, you need to move quickly. Job seekers today are likely to send their resumes to several companies. Assume your candidates also have sent their resumes to your competition. If you spot an attractive resume, reach out immediately! Remember, time kills deals.

STEP 1 is making a qualifying telephone call. It will deliver several benefits. First, it will give you a good "feel" for the candidate's personality. During this call you should ask a few qualifying questions: Are you available to work evenings? Do you have reliable transportation? Remind them that there is a mandatory drug and background test that must be passed. A prospective employee will also likely have several questions for you, too. The point here is to make sure you don't waste time interviewing someone who is not qualified for the position.

STEP 2 is the first face-to-face interview. I always urge those I am about to meet with to relax and be comfortable. Next I remind them that I have numerous questions to ask, adding that at the conclusion of the interview they will be free to ask me any questions about the position. I also let them know up front that I will not make a hiring decision that day, but that I might invite them back for a second interview.

I have found that as an interview begins, it's best to initiate casual conversation about something unrelated to the position or the company; the weather or something related to sports are common "ice-breaker" topics. Doing this helps put them at ease, and gives me some insight into their conversation skills. After several minutes of casual conversation, I will shift to the questions that will help me determine if this candidate is a good fit for our company and our culture. As much as anything, I'm trying to gauge the attitude of the candidate. To me, that's most important.

I also ask questions about other important character traits. **Competitive drive** is very important; I want to know that this candidate is obsessed with winning. I'm also trying to gauge the candidate's **autonomy** and **self-sufficiency**. Because my sales reps usually work alone, I need to be assured they do not need someone to lean on for support throughout the day.

This first interview is the right time to explain in detail the compensation plan. There can be no misunderstanding here. Have the details in writing, so you don't overlook anything. Make sure they know how and when they get paid, when benefits kick in, time-off policies, and whether or not they get paid while in training.

Ideally, you wind up sitting across the desk from a candidate you really like . . . so much so that it's tempting to offer the job right then and there and end the search. Don't! Instead, proceed carefully. You must never appear *too eager* to hire. If you appear to be selling the job, you're apt to scare off a candidate. Those you interview must understand they need you more than you need them. It is OK to sell the dream, just don't sell the job. What do I mean? I let my candidates know about the income potential and opportunity for advancement within the company. But, I also remind them that it takes hard work and a positive attitude to really do well. "If you are an overachiever type," I'll stress, "this *might be* a good opportunity for you."

If I am still interested in hiring this person when the interview concludes, I pose this simple question: "*If I call you back for a second interview, how you would feel about it?"* The response to my question always tells me plenty. Just remember: never appear to be desperate to hire anyone

I recently interviewed a gentleman—I'll call him John—who at first glance appeared to be exactly the person I was looking for. John was very professional in his appearance and in his demeanor. Better yet, as I listened to him answer many of my qualifying questions, I soon realized his attitude was awesome. He had many years of experience outside of my industry, but was very coachable. He also had a great sense of humor. I could tell that having John on my sales staff would be a real pleasure. He appeared to be a perfect fit.

I was itching to offer him the position then and there, but I still followed my own advice: As our interview ended, I asked, "John, if I call you back tomorrow and invite you to return for a second interview, how would you feel about that?" He'd like that very much, he said, and hoped that I would call.

I did, and John has been everything I hoped he would be. Although he has only been on my sales team for a few months, he has been a great addition to our program.

When I do call a candidate back for a second interview is the time I get much more serious about the opportunity at hand. I likely will have another manager sit in to assist in this session. I've even had one of my sales persons come in to help give the candidate more information about the company. If all goes well during this second interview, I will give this prospective employee on a tour of the office, introduce the various personalities, make an offer and—hopefully—get a commitment. If I do, we determine a start date and alert our HR department to prepare all the preemployment paperwork.

TRAIN IN THE FIELD, NOT JUST IN THE OFFICE

You must make sure that every sales consultant is well trained. Indeed, I feel so strongly about training and coaching that I devote an entire chapter to it in the pages that follow. I have found the best way to train a new consultant is by conducting a very organized four- or five-day class. For instance, I have a workbook that each new hire must complete before he or she is ever allowed to go on a sale call. And use your daily sales meetings as opportunities for continuous coaching and training. Identify one step in your sales presentation and train on it. You can never provide too much training.

Field training is essential. I still get out in the field with my sales consultants each week. I relish chances to show off my sales skills, so I really enjoy closing sales and pulling referrals. By working with my team in the field, they see me apply the sales process and techniques that I taught them in the training class. They soon learn how this stuff really works. A lot of sales managers talk about the "good old days" and how they used to close sales. Well, I don't just talk. I highly recommend that you, as a sales manager, shut down your computer and get out in the field with your people. At Certified Security, I made sure not to burden my managers with reports and conference calls, so they could be out in the field several times a week with their reps.

EVALUATE PERFORMANCES MONTHLY

You can't operate at a fast-paced, high-volume level without *monthly* performance evaluations. Yes, *monthly*. Understand, however, that evaluations should never be events a sales reps dread. Nor should it ever be perceived as a "write up," although that could happen if a situation warrants. The evaluation session I envision is a time for a sales manager and a sales consultant to sit down together to discuss in detail the consultant's success. In my monthly meetings with my team members, I always try to give them a positive spin. One of my ongoing goals is to have the sales rep leave the meeting more motivated.

Plenty of performance evaluation forms already exist. But if you cannot find one you like, do what I did: create your own. An evaluation form should include

SIMPLE *fact*

> An action plan is a simple but very detailed plan of specific activities the sales consultant will follow in order to get back on track immediately.

information about what was discussed at the previous meeting, and what improvement was made—or not made. The form should also include a place for the manager to list any necessary actions that should be taken to further improve the consultant's performance. Make sure both you and your consultant sign this document, and be sure the HR department gets a copy for filing.

If a sales consultant is struggling and not meeting the minimum requirements, this is the time to have the sales rep create an action plan. Rather than just issue a warning—"You've got to generate more business and make more sales, or we'll have to part company," have the consultant detail in writing the actions to be taken to get on track. In most cases, the individual knows all too well that failure to follow thru with the plan will result in termination.

An action plan is a simple but very detailed plan of specific activities the sales consultant will follow in order to get back on track *immediately*. It's a plan the consultant creates that the sales manager then approves. Its timeline should be brief, usually no more than 30 days, and the progress should be reviewed by the manager each day. This is a big deal, make no mistake.

SIMPLE
fact

| If you can't measure it, you can't management it.

Not too long ago one of my sales consultants, Bobby, was struggling to pull referrals from the sales he was making. He actually went the entire month and turned in fewer than 30 qualified referrals. During that monthly performance evaluation, I instructed Bobby to come up with an action plan detailing how he was going to get more referrals. The plan he submitted the next day was pretty lame. There were no specifics at all, just a bland promise to ask for more referrals. So Bobby and I sat down to create a real action plan. It included, for instance, his riding with another consultant who was pulling lots of referrals from every sale. We also determined that within one week Bobby would be averaging 10 referrals per sale. I am pleased to report that Bobby hit his goal. Had I not taken corrective action during that monthly evaluation, I'm sure he still would be floundering.

MOTIVATE, MOTIVATE, MOTIVATE!

This, too, is essential, and why there's an entire chapter ahead devoted to motivating your sales staff during daily meetings. Two things to remember: 1) whether you meet daily (as I do) or weekly, start and finish on time, and stay on track; 2) be creative during your meetings, so they don't become predictable, repetitive and *boring*.

Your consultants—and your support staff, too—also need motivation throughout the day. Don't overlook that.

TRACK SALES CAREFULLY

"If you can't measure it, you can't management it."

You must keep track of your prospects, leads, demos no sales, and sales. Whatever resource you use for tracking, by all means keep it simple. Too many managers get buried in the numbers and get off track. Keep the main thing the main thing . . . and the main thing is generating sales.

Inspect what you expect.

SIMPLE
fact

COME TO THE RESCUE

There's nothing more important to your branch than those moments when your sales person is sitting across a table or desk from a prospect and trying to close a sale. As the sales manager, you must be available to help your colleague close the deal.

Before my sales reps can leave any prospect—be it a residence or a business—they must call me, either to: 1) to let me know the prospect was not there and they are leaving the premises; or 2) to ask me how soon we can install the protection (Yippee! We made the sale); or 3) to let me know the prospect has postponed making a buying decision right now. It's this third reason for the call that's especially critical. It gives me a chance to help the sales consultant close the sale by speaking to the prospect myself. That's because I can close about one in three of these "not now" situations.

In truth, my business model is set up for a one-call close for both residential and small business sales—and we consistently close about 80% of prospects on these first calls. In turn, if a sales consultant does leave a prospect without calling me, a "write-up" will almost surely follow. Why am I so hard-nosed? I know from experience that, once a sales consultant leaves a prospect, the chances of us ever getting that sale later on are less than 20%. Enough said.

FOLLOW UP ON ALL DEMO NO SALES

It only takes a few minutes each day to call back the prospects who didn't buy. I first thank each one for allowing us to visit and present our alarm system's capabilities. Then I take a moment or two to ask how my sales consultant did during the presentation. Were we on time for the appointment? Did we answer every question? Were we polite and courteous? finally, though they didn't buy, should I continue to consider them to be a prospect?

The information these calls deliver is very interesting, and helps me determine if I should still consider this prospect a hot lead, which is my No. 1 reason for calling. I've learned, for instance, that one reason why a prospect didn't buy was because the sales person was late for the appointment. Prospects also have told me my reps had been too aggressive. On occasion, I have been able to save deals by sending another sales consultant to meet with them.

MAKE SURE LEAD GENERATION IS A DAILY ACTIVITY

An effective sales manager must know what the sales team is doing each day. *"Inspect what you expect"* applies here, too. It does not take a great deal of time to have your sales team members tell you expressly what they are going to do today to create more sales. And, if a sales consultant cannot quickly tell you what's planned, you've got to be prepared to respond . . . by articulating what you expect to happen today to generate more sales.

SEND ALL INCOMING SALES CALLS TO . . . YOU!

That's right: *you*. It is extremely important that whoever takes responsibility for an incoming sales call be a trained sales person. For this reason I am the only person in the branch who takes that call. We spend plenty of money on both internet advertising and our own website to make the telephone ring. When it does, whoever answers had better be well-trained on how to sell the appointment over the telephone. As we grew at Certified Security, I eventually trained my marketing manager to deal with these calls when I was out in the field and couldn't personally respond. I was fortunate, as well: One of the company owners, Joe Hassan, usually was in the office, too. Joe was one of the best sales person I ever met, and had a special gift for handling these calls. Leave this critical task to a receptionist? Never! I wouldn't even consider it.

In visiting companies around the country as part of the VIP program I offer, I was almost dumbfounded when I heard receptionists trying to set sales appointments. Although these fine ladies (and gentlemen, too) may well have been stalwarts in their companies for many years, they still are not sales persons. No doubt your company, too, is spending plenty of money to make that telephone ring. You've got sales consultants on the street passing out business cards, and you've plastered your telephone number on all your trucks. Make that time, effort and expense pay off. When a prospects calls in, do everything in your power to sell the appointment on the telephone then and there! Which means you truly are the best person to handle the call.

A sales manager's responsibilities may seem overwhelming at times. Indeed, they can be. But those same responsibilities also can deliver abundant rewards. I still love the competitiveness of setting various goals, then reaching them. Watching the individuals on my sales team learn new sales and organizational skills is equally rewarding. If you are a true leader, you understand the joy of watching others do well. To me, the best way to judge the success of a sales leader is not simply by counting how many alarm systems his or her team sold last month, or the number of dollars those systems generated. Rather, it's by assessing on the overall leadership skills the sales manager exhibits, and how the team performs.

> The most important responsibility of the sales manager is to build a sales team.

SIMPLE *fact*

The great thing about leadership is that we all can become more than we are. You and I can continue to improve and continue to help more people.

"I didn't come this far, just to come this far."

A Sales Manager's Areas of Responsibility

The primary responsibility of the sales manager is to manage his or her sales team. This includes building the team, overseeing and appraising its production, and the ensuring morale remains high.

To accomplish this, the sales manager must:

1. Recruit new consultants

    Be constantly looking for good people that could be as asset to the sales team.

2. Interview prospective consultants

3. Hire prospective consultants

    Hiring the right people is almost always one of the manager's most important responsibilities.

4. Watch the training schedule to make sure you coordinate your hiring time with your training schedule.

5. Train—not just in the office, but out in the field

    - Every day in the sales meeting you must chose some area of responsibility to train on. Use role-play and other means of participation to get the best from your daily meeting.

    - Field training is very important. This is usually done in the evenings when you are not tied up in the office. Evaluate consultants on how they are following the steps in the preplanned presentation.

6. Conduct monthly performance evaluations (weekly if necessary)

    New consultants need weekly evaluations, and veterans monthly. Be sure to make a copy of the evaluation; send one to the HR department, and keep a copy in your file for future review.

7. Conduct motivating daily sales meetings

    Each meeting should start on time and should not last more than 45 minutes. In your sales meeting you should always: train, motivate, and recognize achievement. Always be thinking of creative ways to make your meeting interesting.

A Sales Manager's Areas of Responsibility

(continued)

8. Track results carefully

   Keep the sales tracker updated, as well as the media tracker and the daily calendar.

9. Motivate your staff

   You must always maintain a positive "can do" attitude. Motivate the staff throughout the day, not just during the sales meeting.

10. Do turn-overs (assist consultants in closing sales)

    You must be available to assist in closing the sale anytime a consultant is on an appointment.

11. Follow-up on demo no sales

    Call all company provided demo no sales to find out why the customer did not buy.

12. Make sure the consultants are doing some type of lead-generation activity each day

    Be responsible for all incoming media calls.

X _____ Date: _____

Sales Manager

CHAPTER 2

Establish a Culture That is *Obsessed* With Sales

"Office culture will influence profits."

LET'S BEGIN WITH an observation. It's based on my travels around the country visiting companies of all shapes and sizes, conducting workshops and my VIP days program: The significant differences in the attitudes of the respective employees within them were striking. While none of these companies had negative workplace environments, overall employee attitudes in the high-performance sales organizations differed notably from those in what I'll call more traditional ones. How? The organizations turning in big sales numbers seem to eat, sleep and drink sales. It's *all* about sales, every hour of every of every week of every month, year after year.

SIMPLE *fact*

> The organizations turning in the big sales numbers seem to eat, sleep and drink sales.

From the sales consultant on the street to the technician installing the product, everyone is consumed with where the next sale is coming from. These companies realize you can't achieve success just by providing excellent customer service, or by adopting strict policies that everyone must adhere to.

These top sales organizations also understand that generating more sales is not a matter of resorting to fear tactics or by applying more pressure to their sales teams. There is no room in their cultures for that type of motivation. Their employees are more likely to reflect the cheerful attitude of the leadership within the company. In turn, the leaderships and managements know that they, too, must embrace the same sales culture so that it will become the philosophy of the entire office.

As I meet with a company during one of my VIP trips—no matter its size—it does not take long before its culture becomes evident.

Some companies I have visited exhibited a family culture. It is often evident in start-up firms or long-standing small businesses. You also could describe this culture as a "team atmosphere." However, as the company grows and hires diverse personalities, it often becomes very difficult to maintain. To be sure, there is nothing wrong with this culture. In fact, a strong sales leader can kick start this kind of company and give it a sales culture very quickly. For a new sales leader, this can be the opportunity of a lifetime, because its employees usually want to grow. This company is often in the "go-go" stage. It knows it wants more, and wants to compete with the big boys. So it is looking for fresh, new ideas and is open to change.

I found this to be the culture at Scott Alarm Systems when I started there in September 1986. It seemed as if the entire staff were members of Bruce Scott's family. His mother was the receptionist and processed paperwork. His wife handled the book keeping, and his son worked in the central station. Indeed, when I first joined the team there was only two or three employees who were *not* part of the family. My employment application seemed more like *adoption papers*. I was now part of the Scott family. Because Bruce was always thinking big and was a tremendous sales person, that little family business grew to become one of the largest and most respected alarm companies in the nation.

SIMPLE *fact* | Nothing happens until someone sells something.

It doesn't matter if you are a small family-run company, a midsize firm or a large corporate organization. Without a strong sales culture you will never reach your potential in sales, or attract the top producers in your industry.

I have seen companies run by some of the smartest technicians in the industry. They're fine individuals, but without strong sales leadership they just never seem to get it together. Somewhere along the line they decided that just having a clever company name, or having a great-looking sign out front, or a trendy high-profile address that would bring hordes of eager customers to their door would all but guarantee their success. Wrong!

If you are going to make it big in sales, it takes a strong sales culture. And it must start with leadership. If the owner or ranking executive is not a strong sales leader, then it's time to hire one, someone for whom sales is an *obsession*. Other managers must get out of the way and let this leader run the sales team and infect the entire office with his or her obsession with sales.

Assuming you are serious about sales and are ready to commit to having a top-notch, kick-butt, high-performance sales team, here are some suggestions for establishing a great sales culture.

CELEBRATE SALES

Every time a sale is made, make a big deal out of it. In my office now, as it's been in every sales office I have ever run, whenever a sales consultant reports a sale, I sound a siren that everyone hears (and a few may bemoan as ear-splitting). When the siren sounds, you literally can hear the staff down the hall hollering phrases like, *"Hot dog, we just made another sale!"*

When a football running back scores a touchdown, he usually goes crazy: dancing and giving high fives to his teammates. His ultimate goal was to score a touchdown and he did it. Well, the ultimate goal of your sales person is to score a sale. When one hits that goal, why not go a little crazy and celebrate? Hey, enthusiasm is contagious and it's fun. Why do you have to always be so serious at work? Lighten up! Enjoy your team's success! That "score" helps insure everyone in the office has a job next month. As the axiom commands, without sales nothing else happens.

EVERYONE SELLS

Every employee should have this attitude: *I am responsible for sales.* When I worked at Certified Security Systems in Jacksonville, we wanted everyone in the branch to understand that they each were responsible for helping make the next sale. The receptionist understood that her title was really Director of First Impressions. It's why we would never answer an incoming call with any type of answering device. We wanted a charming, smiling voice to answer every call. The person that voice belonged to routinely made the first contact with our new customer, and we wanted to make sure that she understood how important she was to the success of the entire office. We made sure we had someone answering phone calls who could project a smile so bright you could see it through the receiver.

Throughout our Certified Security office we also posted large signs that read, *"Everyone Sells"*.

… and everyone includes your service department; it, too, should be a sales center. The people who handle incoming service calls should have sales training, and every service call should be considered an opportunity to sell additional products and services. Hire the right people to handle service calls, then pay them commissions on the sales they generate.

Service and installation technicians in the field have a great opportunity to sell. Yes, they need training and motivation; but once armed, they can really help create additional profits for your organization.

A PORT IN THE STORM

My sales team members are out in the field several hours each day trying to find new business. When they are out prospecting they hear "No" far more often than "Yes". Indeed, they might hear "No" some 20 to 30 times before they hear even a single "Yes". Along with being bombarded with negative influences all day. So the last thing a sales consultant needs to hear is more negative input when he or she walks in the office. I want my sales team members to be highly respected and appreciated when they are in the branch.

You need to understand that champion sales people are often very emotional creatures. They are easily motivated, but also easily *demotivated*, too—as I once observed first hand. It's a day I will never forget. A young, brand new sales consultant had made his first sale. He was very proud of what he had accomplished. But as he turned in his paperwork to a "sales support" colleague, he was scolded. The forms were not letter-perfect, he was told, "and if you're going to work for this company, you had better get his paperwork right!" the colleague added in scornful tones. Instead of winning praise and a high five for his first sale, the young consultant was humiliated. He was about ready to quit then and there. Ridiculous!

SIMPLE *fact*

> Hire the right people to handle service calls, then pay them commissions on the sales they generate.

Every individual on your staff should understand that its sales people who make everything happen. No, they're hardly perfect. But they are out there on the front line every day, creating business and winning orders so everyone else can have a job. Make your office the port in the storm.

NO OFFICE DRAMA ALLOWED

Be advised: a strong sales force is likely to create some stress within the office. High- powered sales people are not always the best at paperwork; they might be among the worst, in fact. But that's often because top sales people usually tend to be individuals. More often than not, they're not team players. They're all about growth, and trying new things. They tend to push the envelope. In turn, their office may well see them as troublesome mavericks.

Now, I am not about to suggest breaking the rules—or even bending the rules—to accommodate sales people. When problems arise with any member of a sales team, it should be the sole responsibility of the sales manager to deal with that member, not anyone else in some other department.

By the same token, an owner or branch manager needs to make sure everyone in the office understands his or her commitment to sales without allowing anyone else feeling subordinate or less important. Everyone needs to understand they have a part in the sales process.

HIRE CHAMPION SALES PEOPLE

Your sales team should be one of positive sales consultants: men and women who can be easily motivated and readily embrace your sales objectives. Once you have surrounded yourself with these overachievers . . . turn up the heat. Set guidelines and demand excellence just as soon as they understand your program. And do not for one minute tolerate laziness or bad attitudes from anyone. Prune these people from your team quickly.

Now, all of this takes a strong sales leader. A sales team will never be more enthusiastic or exciting than the sales manager

> Do not for one minute tolerate laziness or bad attitudes from anyone. Prune these people from your team quickly.

SIMPLE
fact

is. Being the sales leader also means being the sales team's cheerleader, and totally buying into the organization's sales culture. A sales manager who does not understand the importance of a strong sales culture is the wrong person for the job. At the same time, an enthusiastic sales leader can have a huge influence on developing and maintaining the sales culture in the office.

A sales manager has specific responsibilities, too. But that's a topic for another chapter.

LIVE THE CULTURE

A strong, robust sales culture delivers ample benefits, starting with your bottom line. A true sales culture will increase it, plain and simple. In one study I read, companies with a strong sales culture earned much higher profits than those with a traditional or corporate culture. Second—and important in its own right—a sales culture is simply more fun. The office staffs at these companies seem to smile more, which definitely made those offices more exciting places to work.

If you are serious about sales, understand first and foremost that you are a sales organization. Being one is Job 1. If the organization's leadership embraces that attitude, so will everyone else. And it will spread the sales culture throughout the office.

Bates Security in Lexington KY. Enjoys a group outing at the YMCA

CHAPTER 3

Need a Little Inspiration? Come to Meetin'

"The greatest leader is not necessarily the one who does the greatest things. He is the one that gets the people to do the greatest things."—Ronald Reagan

Brace yourself. What you're about to read may strike you as preposterous.

There is still no better spark for igniting and motivating a sales team than an effective sales meeting. Yes, you read correctly—and notice I've written *effective sales meeting*.

> For the high performance sales team, conference call sales meetings are a colossal waste of time.

SIMPLE *fact*

It's a critical distinction. I further contend that a well-planned sales meeting also remains the very best way to kick off a new sales contest or campaign, or revive a sales team and get it back on track when production seems flat and morale a little down.

I have been leading sales meetings for over 25 years, and mine have been effective, productive and time incredibly well-spent. I'm hardly alone in my thinking. The value of an effective sales meeting is well understood by every successful sales organization in my industry, and most other industries. And if you will follow the simple blueprint I am about to present, your sales meetings, too, can become dynamic sessions that your people will actually enjoy and look forward to, because of the fresh excitement they will generate and the success that follows.

I know what I'm about to submit goes against the grain. Indeed, the very word "meeting" can make eyes roll, arouse sighs of discontent, or provoke murmurs of, "Oh, no! Not *another* meeting." I also know all too well that there's good reason for such derision. I still can recall a leadership meeting I attended at a major company, and hearing its president ask a group of sales managers how often they held sales meetings. As we went around the room and each manager answered, I was astounded at what I heard next:

- "Weekly meetings that might last for a few hours," was a common reply.
- "Once a month," replied a few others.
- "As needed," was another response, while one or two of these so-called "sales leaders" said the sales meetings they convened were really "conference calls."

No wonder sales results were lagging, I concluded silently as I listened. These managers had no idea about what a sales meeting was supposed to accomplish, much less know how to run an effective one.

That's not the kind of sales meeting I'm about to describe and recommend. So stay with me and keep an open mind. What I am about to present to you probably does run counter to conventional wisdom, or what you've experienced. But your reward will be learning about techniques you can use to run a great sales meeting and further develop championship sales professionals.

Let's start with a frequently asked the question, and my first contention that might rub you the wrong way: *How often should a manager conduct a sales meeting?*

Every day! Five days a week.

Yes, you read that correctly, too. if you are going to run a high-powered, take-no-prisoners, juggernaut of a successful sales organization, that's my first recommendation: Meet with your sales team *daily.*

Now before you go conjuring up all the reasons why that's just not possible, let me tell you this: I do it today with my team, just as I've been meeting with my sales teams for more than 20 years. It can be done, despite the litany of excuses I've also heard for more than 20 years.

Among the laments is: "My people live too far from the office and cannot possibly be at the office every morning." My response to this one is simple: Don't hire anyone who cannot meet for a daily sales meeting. For instance, when we started assembling our high-volume sales team in the Fort Lauderdale branch of Certified Security, we had lots of great applicants from such locales as South Miami and North Palm Beach County. We discarded these resumes in the blink of an eye, because I did not want anyone on my team who could not be part of our daily sales meetings. It helped drive home how important they are—and that there is no one so important that he or she may be excused from attending them.

Another lament came from a company vice president: sales managers did not like convening sales meetings daily. So what!? I asked crisply. I didn't always like holding daily meetings with my team, either, but I realized they were necessary to get everyone motivated for what needed to be accomplished.

Another excuse is the notion that a daily a sales meeting wastes time that would be better spent by getting team members out in the field for more hours. Well, an even greater waste of time will result if those hours out in the field aren't spent productively.

Conducting a sales meeting via a conference call doesn't cut it, either. Nice try, but while you, the manager, are trying to motivate the team during your conference call, your teammates are apt to be playing solitaire or checking Facebook. Face it: We've all been on conference calls and have been totally distracted from what was being discussed. Conference call sales meetings are a colossal waste of time. The odds of motivating anyone are mighty slim. At best, about all you can do is give out information. Can you imagine a football coach getting all the players together on a *conference call* before a big game to discuss a new play or to get the team fired up? Neither can I. How can a leader motivate the troops if he or she does not meet face-to-face with the troops?

What's the real reason many managers resist scheduling sales meetings? Because they simply don't know how to plan them, or they're not sure what to do or say once they convene the meeting. But that's a lousy justification for not meeting at all. In certain situations, yes, I'll concede that a sales manager might get by with a weekly

meeting instead of a daily one. But that weekly meeting had better be one great session, and packed with motivation and accountability.

Daily or weekly, whenever a sales meeting is scheduled it needs to be a big event. Get everyone on the team together in one place, rally the team, and identify what's needed to get the job done. Planning a dynamic sales meeting is not difficult. To have a successful sales meeting, you only need to accomplish three things.

1. TRAIN YOUR PEOPLE

A sales manager needs to use the sales meeting as an opportunity to provide valuable information to the sales team that will help them close more business. Championship sales pros are prospecting all the time. They need continuous training. There are new products and services that need to be discussed, and training to demonstrate how and when to present new technology. Think about the steps in your sales presentation; pick any of those steps and train on that process. Present the best ideas for: overcoming objections, generating appointments, creating needs among clients, writing a thank-you note, and how to ask for referrals.

SIMPLE *fact* | A sales meeting is not the place to embarrass anyone.

I probably focus on referrals at least three to four times a month. The list of training topics is almost endless.

- **Role playing.** It's an effective training tool for any meeting. To make the role play more effective, be sure to alert the role-play participants ahead of time, so they'll be prepared. Keep a light-hearted attitude during the activity, too. By having fun while training helps create a comfortable environment. A sales meeting is not the place to embarrass anyone.

- **Plan ahead.** A sales manager must be well-prepared for a meeting's training exercises. I usually make a list of training topics a week in advance. After each day's meeting I review what the topic will be for the next day, so I can be thinking and preparing throughout the day.

- **Don't be predictable.** Get creative by using different people to lead some of the training. If you have sales consultants who have certain skills, harness them at your meetings. Remember, one of the basic rules of leadership is: "*Don't do anything that one of your subordinates can do 85% as well as you can.*"

2. MOTIVATE YOUR PEOPLE

Keep it positive. I always start my meetings with fairly loud motivational music. I want to begin with excitement. I will never allow anyone in the room to erode the excitement level I am trying to create. Positive success stories only! Do not discuss anything negative that happened in the past. When I was the sales manager at Certified Security Systems in Jacksonville, I always kept a spray can of Lysol close by. If anyone in the meeting began spewing any negative comments or stories, I'd instantly call "Time out!" Then I sprayed the Lysol toward the source of the negative junk. No negative talk allowed in my meetings! None!

Every sales manager needs to get out the message: "Today is a new day with brand new opportunities." *Enthusiasm sells,* just like on a sale call. A sales manager also serves as the meeting's cheerleader. Keep the energy level high. The sales consultants will be as positive or excited as the manager is no more, no less. The excitement and enthusiasm a sales manager expresses will be contagious. Want an excited, motivated sales team? Then get excited and show it.

Sales consultants are in the field all the live long day. And the most successful ones are meeting people all the live long day, too.

> Want an excited, motivated sales team? Then get excited and show it.

SIMPLE *fact*

The majority of those people will likely give them some type of negative response. Hearing "No" for much of any day is tough to endure. So the last thing a sales team needs is to first sit through a negative sales meeting. When the team arrives for a sales meeting, it ought to be greeted with smiles and high fives for a job well done.

Update the scoreboard before the sales meeting. Every sales room should have a sales tracking board. This is your team's scoreboard. An effective manager understands that championship sales people are usually very competitive and want to see the results of their success posted for their peers to see. Accommodate them. And be sure the tracking board is updated daily.

Use sales contests as motivators. A great contest not only can be fun, but it also can create interest among a sales force. Here are a few guidelines I use when designing one:

- **Have a contest everyone can win**. Every spring Daytona Beach, Florida, celebrates "Bike Week". Thousands of bikers from all over the country make the trip on motorcycles (naturally!) to show off and party. During that same week I thought it would be a good idea to have our own "Bike Week" contest. We bought a beautiful Schwinn 15-speed bicycle that was worth almost $2,000. The rules were simple: Whoever turned in the most referrals in one week won the bike. The first few days were great. Sales were up, with referrals coming in from every sale. There was just one problem: Eli Veydt, one of my reps, got so excited he started pulling in 40 to 50 referrals . . . from every sale! Well, soon it was obvious who was going to win my contest. Everyone on the team quit trying and watched Eli, who turned in almost 500 referrals. I learned my lesson. Ever since, every contest I've designed makes it possible for every team member reaching the goal to win the big prize.

- **Keep it brief.** A short contest is usually more successful than a month-long contest because it will provide immediate gratification. If you are running a contest for more than one week, make sure to keep everyone updated on the results several times a day. If you don't, your sales people likely will lose focus.

- **Keep it simple.** If the contest seems complicated, a sales team will not get excited about it.

- **Make it an obsession.** If you are going to have a contest, make it a big deal. Decorate the room. Design a scoreboard that reflects its theme. Above all, have fun celebrating the contest's results.

- **Be the leader of the contest.** The contest will never be more exciting than the manager makes it. Keep the results in front of your team and keep them excited. I think the results of a sales contest is a pretty good reflection on the leadership of the sale manager.

SIMPLE *fact*

A well-planned sales meeting also remains the very best way to kick off a new sales contest or campaign, or revive a sales team and get it back on track when production seems flat and morale a little down.

You can read more about about seven of the sales contests I created in the Appendix at the back of this book, including the rules I established and the rewards.

Have fun during your meeting. During my sales manager years at Certified Security we played Bingo with the sales team about every two weeks. Beforehand, I'd always go to a toy store and purchase a simple Bingo game to use in the office. In our meeting I would pass out one Bingo card to everyone on the sales team. And If, say, Sally and Jim had each made sales the preceding day, they would each get an addition card. I also would invite Joe Hassan, our company owner, to be the Certified Bingo caller. We would joke around a lot, and make a big deal out of each number called out. The first few winners of the Bingo game would receive a $20 gas card or perhaps the next company lead. Silly? Probably. But this little contest always fired the team up and was a really great source of motivation and fun. During one session we had one sales rep so excited that he actually did a back flip in the sales room when he won!

3. RECOGNIZE YOUR PEOPLE'S ACHIEVEMENTS

Be sure to celebrate success: Have one or two of your consultants who have closed a big sale, or who had to deal with an especially tough prospect to close the sale, tell their stories. Let them brag about their success in front of their sales peers. Accountability is an important part of every sale person's responsibility. I recommend that sales managers always ask team members to individually announce their results from the previous sale period—but also be sure *not* to publically embarrass anyone by calling them out individually for any lack of success.

> A well-planned sales meeting should be a time of motivation and excitement.

SIMPLE *fact*

Never scold publicly. A sales meeting is neither the time or place for reprimanding your sales team. Remember: *"Praise in public, chastise in private."* Look for reasons to give your team praise during your meeting. It might be one team member's first sale; or perhaps a consultant sold one of the new products or services just included in a recent offer.

After every touchdown, the player who scored wants to celebrate. So help your team members "spike the ball" after scoring by making their victories big deals. In my sales meetings, any sales reps who reports three sales in one day gets a 15-second standing ovation during the next sales meeting. And deservedly so. I have seen motivational sales meetings destroyed by a few cutting remarks from the manager or owner. If a sales person made a mistake or did something contrary to company policy, do not announce it in front of his or her peers. That is a discussion held behind closed doors.

A well-planned sales meeting should be a time of motivation and excitement. It's when the team gets in the huddle before the big play and comes up with a strategy to score big.

Here are more tips to help you plan and stage a great meeting:

- Start on time
- Stop on time
- Be well prepared: Have an agenda for your meeting and stick with it; don't get sidetracked
- Make the meeting interesting to everyone
- Keep the meeting moving
- Stay on topic

- Use your people in the meeting
- Watch your personal appearance
- Don't use the meeting as an opportunity to "beat up" your team or an individual
- Be an enthusiastic leader in the meeting
- Have fun!

CHAPTER 4

The Four Stages in the Life of a Sales Person

If your past ever becomes more important to you than your future goals and dreams, you are in trouble.

I COULDN'T BEGIN to count all the sales consultants I have trained over the years. There have been thousands. Many of them went on to become very successful, and remain a source of personal pride and satisfaction. On occasion, of course, some others wound up being terminated, or quit on their own only after a few days of training.

There are various reasons why some flourish and others fail. Obviously, individual attitudes have a tremendous influence on success. Other factors could be the quality of leadership in the office, office culture, the quality and amount of training, and unexpected changes in company policy or products. And, now and then, a manager just makes a bad hire; nobody's hiring track record is perfect.

A professional sales leader continually keeps a keen eye on every sales consultant. The leader watches carefully to make sure that each one remains motivated, and does not get discouraged. It's critically important for the leader to understand how his or her sales team members are likely to go through various stages during their employment. A leader who fails to pay attention to sales consultants' attitudes can often lead to someone on the team developing a bad attitude that spreads to the other teammates. As often as not, the negative attitude results in someone quitting or getting fired—and that someone who departed may once have been the sales team's top producer.

SIMPLE
fact

The success or failure of a sales consultant, many times is a direct reflection on the leadership skills of the sales manager.

As I assessed my years of training, coaching and leading sales teams, I have concluded that you can divide the professional life of a sales consultant's career into four stages. Describing each of them in detail is the focus of this chapter. All four stages are shaped by three factors: **enthusiasm, motivation** and **competence**. A sales person moving from one stage to another is the result of the changes in these factors. As I describe these stages, chances are you will be able to identify someone on your sales team or in your organization who personifies one of them.

Employee Production Cycle

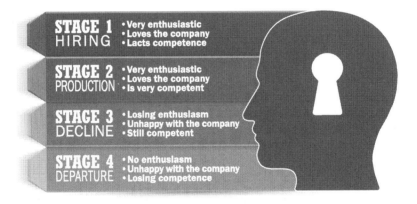

STAGE 1
HIRING
• Very enthusiastic
• Loves the company
• Lacts competence

STAGE 2
PRODUCTION
• Very enthusiastic
• Loves the company
• Is very competent

STAGE 3
DECLINE
• Losing enthusiasm
• Unhappy with the company
• Still competent

STAGE 4
DEPARTURE
• No enthusiasm
• Unhappy with the company
• Losing competence

STAGE 1: THE HIRING

I also call this the Honeymoon Stage. The new sales consultant—let's call her Marcia—is just beginning her relationship with the company. Everything is beautiful in her eyes. She cannot find fault with anything. She is telling everyone about her new job and how great the company is. Marcia's **enthusiasm** at this stage is off the charts. She sees her new position as a new adventure, a new chapter in her life. She is absolutely committed to success.

Marcia is also **highly motivated**, in part because during the hiring process you convinced her she can indeed do the job.

At the same, Marcia is not very **competent**. Upon her joining your sales staff, you spent a few days training her on your product, and company policy and procedures, but she still has plenty to learn. She is making mistakes, but can be forgiven because of all the activity she is engaged in.

At this stage your new sales consultant is "fired up" and ready to make things happen. For the time being, Marcia also will be your biggest fan. As her supervisor you are someone she enjoys working for. The first month or so in a sales person's career often can be most successful, fueled solely by enthusiasm and motivation. I once had a new hire who made more sales in his first week in the field than any other sales consultant in the office. His confidence level was extremely high. His paperwork was terrible, but we tolerated because he was making sales.

Throughout this first stage, which usually lasts a week or 10 days, a new sale consultant like Marcia is going to be working very closely with her manager. In turn, her manager must be prepared to spend time with her, both in training and in the field.

STAGE 2: PRODUCTION

During this stage your new sales consultant is still **very enthusiastic**. Marcia still loves coming to work every day. She remains excited about almost everything and is still making sales. Moreover, she also is setting some goals. And, she now understands that sales people are not born; they're made.

> The first month or so in a sales person's career often can be most successful, fueled solely by enthusiasm and motivation.

SIMPLE *fact*

Marcia's level of **motivation** is still very high, too. She is starting to make money, and in her eyes this is the "real deal." She might even be thinking about her next step in the chain of command. Similarly, her internal drive is high . . . which means her manager does not have to worry at all about his still-new hire goofing off during the work day.

There are several qualities that I typically observe in such top performers at this stage:

- **A SENSE OF URGENCY.** There is no place for complacency in their work lives. Champion sales people understand that waiting for leads or business to land in their laps is a total waste of time. It does not matter how successful they might have been yesterday; today is a new day. So these high performers realize they must be proactive every day.

- **GREAT CONFIDENCE.** It appears in three areas. First, they believe their *company* is beyond a doubt the best in the area. Second, they are confident their *product* is superior to the competition's. Finally, they are feeling really good about *themselves*.

- **VERY ORGANIZED.** Being organized begins with maintaining a daily planner. Top producers do it faithfully. The job-description form my sales consultants sign states plainly that each must have and maintain a day planner or some electronic scheduling device. Occasionally during sales meetings I will ask to see the planners. Because so much follow-up is required, it's mandatory for every successful sales consultant to have their respective schedules at their fingertips.

- **PERPETUALLY PROACTIVE.** It's almost the "flip-side" of being well-organized. Being proactive means that every day the sales rep is doing something to create new business. This activity includes cold calling on businesses, calling existing clients, calling referrals, sending thank-you notes to those they have called upon, and working with power partners that can send them business.

SIMPLE *fact*

> Champion sales people understand that waiting for leads or business to land in their laps is a total waste of time.

Marcia's **competency level** is now high. In part, that's because she is making many right decisions on her own. She no longer leans on her manager for as much help or support as she did in stage one. Indeed, at this level Marcia might even be able to help her manager conduct some training. She can be counted on to run the sales meeting if the sales team manager is on vacation. She has a pretty solid grasp of the company's products and is very comfortable embracing new products.

So what's the manager's most critical job now? It should be clear: *Do everything possible to keep the entire sales team in this stage!* It goes without saying how much easier a sales manager's job will be if everyone on the team keeps working at this stage. It will enable the manager, too, to be more productive—and more creative. Better still, this stage of a sales consultant's life will continue as long as a manager can keep that consultant motivated and enthusiastic. In fact, a sales manager's ability to keep team members at the production stage is a mighty good test of the manager's overall leadership capabilities.

STAGE 3: LOSS OF ENTHUSIASM & MOTIVATION

For some reason, things now don't seem to be going so well for Marcia. It's not that unusual, either. An effective sales manager will readily recognize small weaknesses and factors that can fester and morph into big problems. If ignored, though,

Marcia's steady **decline in enthusiasm** soon will become obvious to everyone on her sales team.

She is **not as motivated** as she was up until a few weeks ago. Her production has declined, and she seems to be finding fault with the product or the company, or both. She is not showing up on time for meetings; when she is on hand, she might even be openly critical during discussions. Several factors can cause a sales consultant to slide—or stumble—into this stage.

> An effective sales manager will readily recognize small weaknesses and factors that can fester and morph into big problems.

SIMPLE *fact*

- *Change.* Something happened that flipped positive perceptions and outlooks into negatives. And left Marcia thinking, "This isn't how it was when I was hired."
- Broken promises.
- Negative input from someone else in the office.
- Lack of support.
- Payroll issues.
- Personal problems that cause the sales rep to become distracted.
- Time off for vacations or to address health issues.

Marcia still **seems to be competent**. You could describe her as "OK," and conclude she still "gets it." Yet, her production is noticeably lower and her attitude is generally sour.

In my early days as a rookie sales manager, I made the mistake of not dealing with a person in this stage. I also spent a lot of time worrying about his production. I wound up losing this team member who at one time had been my top producer—and when he quit he took another sales rep with him. Instead of bringing him in and working with him, I ignored the situation and kept hoping things would just get better. Well, they didn't, and I learned a lesson the hard way: Problems like this one do not fix themselves. They must be met head-on and corrected.

At this point, then, Marcia's manager must deal with her immediately. If her behavior continues, a fourth and final stage is inevitable. Worse, her negative attitude is contagious, and can spread throughout the sales team and wreck others' production as it spreads.

STAGE 4: LOSS OF ENTHUSIASM & MOTIVATION . . . AND LOSS OF COMPETENCE

Once a sales consultant's enthusiasm and motivation withers and dies, the loss of competence almost inevitably follows. Marcia's infectious negative attitude simply cannot be tolerated. You cannot keep her on your staff in her condition. By allowing this kind of personality to remain, you are sending a message to her peers and office colleagues that you have low standards and expectations. Something has to change, and right away.

Take, for example, a sales team member I'll refer to as Ralph. He quickly became our sales office record-setter. Ralph took very few company leads, but it seemed he didn't need to, since he sold lots of additional products on just about every deal. After a few months, though, Ralph developed a negative attitude. Then he lost his motivation. I tried to work with him, but he continued to rebel. Ralph was always telling me how the competition sold, and how much better it was. After only a few days of this rebellious nature, I actually gave Ralph the name phone number of someone I knew at one of my competitors, and told him to call them. He would fit in nicely over there, I added pointedly. Now Ralph is that competitor's problem—since I gave him that phone number while I was terminating him.

SIMPLE *fact*

Anytime you lose an employee, ask yourself this question; "Was the reason we lost this person my fault or their fault?"

Managers need to remember: regardless of how much production a sales person might deliver, your rule had better be that *no one* holds you hostage. There is not one person on your sales team good enough to be a negative influence on your team's other members. Not ever. Keeping Ralph would have sent a signal to my entire office that he was in control, and that I was a weak manager. At times you simply have to cut your losses. Ralph was one of those times.

OK, so how do you, as the sale leader, make sure that all your Marcias stay in the production stage, and no one becomes a Ralph?

Here are a few ideas that work for me:

- **Daily motivation:** Remind your team members that they are doing a good job and are greatly appreciated.
- **Correct any negativity immediately**: Don't let even one bad attitude fester. Resolve it, one way or another.

- **Coach continuously**: Once you have trained your new sales consultant, do not throw him or her to the wolves. There's lots more coaching to do along the way. Withholding it will usually result in a negative attitude.

- **Give them attention:** Text messages and/or phone calls throughout the day enables you to stay in touch, and remind team members that you care enough to monitor their progress. Touching base goes a long way every day.

  > Regardless of how much production a sales person might deliver, your rule had better be that no one holds you hostage.

  SIMPLE *fact*

- **Make sure they stay busy with proactive activity:** Every day you need to make sure your sales consultants are busy hunting new business. If they do not each have proactive activity scheduled for the day assign them one. A daily purpose and goal is paramount.

- **Evaluate performance**: I meet with each person on my sales team, one-on-one, for a performance evaluation each month. A new consultant will likely meet with me every week for a few months. In the pages ahead, I will review what a successful performance evaluation is all about. For now, just know it's a great motivational tool.

- **Lighten up!** Make your office or sales room a fun place to be. Enough said

CHAPTER 5

Getting Your Team To Buy Into Your Vision and Goals

"If your actions inspire others to dream more, learn more, do more and become more, you are a leader." —John Quincy Adams

IN 1898 A French naturalist, Jean Henri Fabre, demonstrated the unusual behavior of the processionary caterpillar. What Fabre found especially interesting was its instinct to follow directly behind the caterpillar in front of it. This behavior is what gives the caterpillar its name.

Fabre placed a number of them in single file around the top rim of a flower pot. Each caterpillar's head touched the back end of the one in front of it. After lining up the caterpillars, Fabre placed pine straw in the flower pot just a few inches from where they were lined up. Pine straw happens to be these caterpillars' favorite food.

The caterpillars began following each other around the top of the pot, thinking they were headed to the food. They kept following each other around the top of the flower pot . . . for seven days! After one week, they started to drop dead from this mindless activity. These insects literally starved to death with their life-sustaining food just inches away. They were locked into a lifestyle and could not break themselves free from their instinctive behavior.

I too often see sales consultants who seem to be no different than these caterpillars. They have the ability to change their direction in life, but seem to be locked into a lifestyle of mindless activities. These consultants are busy enough, but often confuse activity with achievement. They appear to be caught up in a vicious circle of going nowhere.

SIMPLE *fact*

> You really cannot set goals for your team. Your team members have to set goals for themselves.

A few months ago I was working with the sales team of a large company. The owner and the manager both expressed to me how their sales team seemed to be in a rut. This leadership team seemed to have very good goals in mind, ones that lined up perfectly with their business model. But they were having a difficult time getting their sales people to get with the program. It soon became clear to me that their sales team members didn't share the leadership team's goals. By the time I arrived, the company's leaders were at wits' end trying to get everyone on the same page. Their frustration prompted two questions:

1. *"How can we get our sales people to buy in to our goals for the year?"*

2. *"How can we get our sales people to conduct lead-generation activity each day?"*

Both are great questions. In preparing my responses, I thought about the sales teams I had coached in the past. How had I convinced my teams to buy in to my goals? What had I done that led them to grasp the numerous benefits of creating new business each day?

Yes, I was convincing. And if I could be, so can you. As I declared in this book's opening pages, when performed correctly the sales manager's job is the branch's toughest. Trying to motivate diverse personalities while keeping everyone focused continually on the same agenda is no easy task. Once I shaped and articulated the goals for my teams, it still took quite a bit of sweat, toil and persuasion to unite all my individual consultants in pursuit of a common cause.

The effort always began by keeping in mind this rock-solid truth: *You* really cannot set goals for your team. *Your team members* have to set goals for themselves. To get this done, you must carefully motivate them to achieve the goal you hope they will embrace.

While I was the sales manager at Certified Security Systems in Jacksonville, company owner Joe Hassan would routinely ask me for my sales goals for a given month or quarter. Each December, for example, I could count on Joe bugging me about my goals for the next year's first quarter. In a way, I bugged him back: I always avoided giving Joe a direct answer until after I had first met with my sales team. You see, if I set the goal, it would not be the team's goal, but one I had set for it. And, having set a goal for

SIMPLE
fact

my team, I would then have to go and first sell it to its members . . . and hope that everyone would individually commit to helping achieve it. That's not what I wanted.

Instead, I first met with my sales team and challenged it to think about what might be possible. Next, I would get team members' individual goals. To be sure, if what they told me did not match up to what I was hoping to hear—or if the totals I got back were ridiculously too high or too low—I went back to work and spent more time challenging everyone to get it right.

A cynic may accuse me of splitting hairs here, but it was a sincere and effective exercise, and it did deliver results. Here are the concepts that enabled me to achieve our goals, and the buy-in I was after:

SIMPLE
fact

You need to paint a picture to show each team member not only what's possible but how everyone can realize the possibilities.

1. **First, understand there are two elements required for growth: change and commitment.** We all want to improve, and we all talk about setting goals. That's the easy stuff. If you are serious about a goal and growth, you had better prepare a plan of attack. You are not going to grow naturally. There must be a change, and there must be *commitment to the change.* You must carefully decide what changes you are going to make. Are you going to hire more sales people? Adjust your price structure? Switch to a new or different product line? One company I advised decided to launch an advertising campaign.

   Whatever changes you opt for, you must then commit to see the change through. Don't not make any change if you are not willing to commit to it. And, know that any commitment requires your setting some serious goals right away.

2. **Carefully share the goal or vision with the sales team.** Early on, share your commitment with your sales people. Stress with them the new direction the company is about to take, and what it encompasses—and then

remind your team members how attaining the resulting goal is largely up to them.

3. **Create a plan to reach that goal**. Setting a goal is the first step toward hitting it. Then the real work begins. There must be a detailed plan for reaching this goal. I made sure that before I asked each person for individual goals I laid out a plan of action. After I explained how we were going to reach for new heights, I then individually asked team members what they felt like they could contribute toward hitting a new goal I had in mind.

4. **Motivate your team to get it excited about the goal.** Here again, sales goals ultimately must come from your team's members. If you force goals on them, they will never buy-in. And, yes, you'll undoubtedly need to put your motivational skills to work to muster the excitement about reaching the goal. But that's what selling is all about.

5. **Team members must believe that they can attain the goal.** This is where your leadership ability counts most. You need to paint a picture to show each team member not only what's possible but how *everyone* can realize the possibilities.

6. **What's in it for them?** You must be able to explain to how team members will individually benefit from reaching the goal. Most often, it's all about the money.

7. **Goals must be based on individual potential**. For example, if your new sales consultant Marcia sets a goal that clearly is beyond her potential, you'll need to reel her back to reality. Have Marcia adjust the goal to make sure it's one she will be able to attain.

8. **Be specific and well-defined.** No fluff here! Never allow someone to say a goal is to "work harder" or to "get more referrals" or "make more calls." Anyone who offers that kind of response in this context is not taking this exercise serious. Goals must be specific. My reply to someone who throws out this kind of lame objective is, "OK. So you say you are going to work harder. Exactly what do you mean by that?"

9. **Remind them that you will hold them accountable.** You must be specific here, too. A fundamental of goal-setting is establishing

SIMPLE
fact

> Never allow someone to say a goal is to "work harder" or to "get more referrals" or "make more calls."

a time line. How and when are you going to be holding team members accountable for hitting their goals?

10. **Remind each team member that it's more than just a goal**. It's a *commitment*. You truly believe everyone on your team can achieve (or even exceed) their respective goals, and you are expecting each of them to be successful.

11. **Never adjust the finish line**. A national company whose name you would know realized one

> Do not adjust your goal. Adjust your people.

SIMPLE *fact*

September that it was not going to even come close to hitting its yearly sales goal. So it simply moved the goal closer so it could look better. It didn't fool anyone, and the organization wound up looking worse. *Do not adjust your goal!* Adjust your people. You need to monitor very closely the progress that each person on your team is making. Don't wait until the third quarter of the game to start motivating. As New England Patriots coach Bill Belichick once advised, "If you wait until halftime to adjust, it's too late." His wisdom applies to selling, too. If you see someone on your team falling behind early, you need to work with that person immediately, and leave the target alone. When you move the target, you damage morale and show weakness. **Increase activity; don't ever move the target.**

SIMPLE *fact*

> Getting your team to buy in to your vision and embrace your goals is always going to require your taking the time and effort to motivate your team members.

I have been in too many goal-setting meetings that were all fluff. Typically, the fluff started flying as the manager went around the room asking for individual goals. Since nobody was about to risk being embarrassed, each person tossed out an objective without any regard to unavoidable circumstances that might erupt. Everyone in the room knew there was no way anyone was likely to hit the targets being expressed. At the time, everyone felt good. But that was as far as it went. It was a total waste of time.

Getting your team to buy in to your vision and embrace your goals is always going to require your taking the time and effort to motivate your team members. They must have a clear understanding of the benefits of your vision, what you want your team to achieve, and how. Get the message across that reaching the goal will be of benefit to them both individually and as a team, and you will instill pride in their capabilities and unite them for the cause.

CHAPTER 6

Motivating Your Sales Team

I don't want to just compete. I want to dominate.

SALES PEOPLE HAVE a tough job. In fact, I can't think of a tougher job, because accompanying it is an ever-present burden: It's the sales reps who are saddled with the responsibility of finding business . . . so everyone else in the office will have a job.

SIMPLE *fact*

> I believe successful sales people should be well paid.

Forget about any perceived glamour. Sales is hard on the ego. It requires a lot of energy. Top producers are prospecting every day, and if their peers followed their example, they'd be top producers, too. Sales people have to understand and learn to react instantly to what their customers tell them. Sales people are told "No!" far more often than they're told, "Yes!" For these reasons alone—and I could cite others—I believe successful sales people should be well paid. In many organizations the top sales producers are the highest-paid employees; as it should be, I contend.

Sales people have different skill sets. Some excel at prospecting and identifying new customers. Others excel at closing the sale. Still others I worked with over the years did not generate as many sales as others on the team, but made more money because they were great at selling additional products and services. In turn, their commission on each sale was higher.

To be a good sales manager, you need to know the respective skills of your team members. It is also important to understand that sales people are not all motivated by the same things. So it is critical for you, as the sale leader, to identify what excites your individual team members, be it cash . . . gifts . . . prestige . . . recognition of a job well-done . . . or job satisfaction. I can assure you of this: the superstars on your team _want_ to be on top. They want to _win_!

It's the sales manager's job to help them win: to both achieve maximum production and reach their maximum potential. Of all the responsibilities a sales manager must shoulder, motivating the sales team had better be near the top of the list. As the sales leader, it's up to you to determine how best to fire up each individual personality on your team, and get the very best from each person every day, every week, every month throughout the year.

SIMPLE _fact_ | Sales people can be both easy to motivate and easy to demotivate.

How you motivate is your call, since you should know your teammates and their personalities better than anyone else. Just be sure that _accountability_ is part of your motivational strategy. Also be aware of two more key factors: first, understand that the best sales people are usually more emotional than other office employees. They can be both easy to motivate and easy to _demotivate_. Second, be aware of the strong influences the spouses of your sales consultants can be, given their very natural interest in seeing their husbands and wives succeed.

I have seen some sales managers who were just cheerleaders. They tried motivating the team only with high energy, but never held anyone accountable. Then there are the managers who were bull-dog tough, hammered their teams relentlessly, and wielded fear continuously. There is no question that fear often can be the greatest motivator. But only for a short time, and it comes at a high price. If you continually use fear and scare tactics to drive results, you'll burn out your team and suffer very low morale. To me, fear is not a long-term motivator, and it certainly is not conducive to a fun atmosphere than every sales organization needs.

The tools that I use to keep my teams motivated include these:

- **High commissions.** For most sales consultants, they're easily the No. 1 motivator. I talk about commissions often when conferring with my sales people. During a sales meeting, for example, I'll routinely ask a consultant how much money he or she made on a big sale. I want everyone on the team to know how one of their peers is making big money. When someone on the team hits a bonus level, I send out a text message to everyone congratulating the sales consultant for the achievement.

- **Immediate gratification.** I want my sales people to be paid as quickly as possible, since most sales people prefer it. As a rule, your most aggressive sales reps are not long-term planners. They respond best when the reward is immediate. It's why sales contests that last for more than a week or so usually are not very successful. If your company's pay cycle is more than two weeks, it will be more of a challenge to motivate them with financial compensation.

- **Keep score.** Because your "top guns" are very competitive, keeping an

> Sales people love to brag about winning the sale.

SIMPLE *fact*

updated sales scoreboard in the sales room is critical. Keep it simple, too, so sales reps can see at a glance how they stack up with their peers. They *do* want to know: I've heard reps tell me how it really wasn't important to them to be on the top the board . . . and in the next breath complain because they thought the board hadn't posted one of their sales. Yes, they do want to win!

- **Public recognition.** To some reps, it ranks as high as commissions. Use every opportunity to praise your individual sales consultants. In my years as sale manager at Certified Security Systems, one of the company's owners often would sit in my sales meeting. I would always leverage that opportunity and have someone on the team crow a little about a sale success from the preceding day. It proved to be a great motivational tool. Sales people love to brag about winning the sale . . . and having something to show for it. A top producer on one of my teams was motivated by trophies. For him, it's wasn't, "Show me the money!" as much as it was, "Show me the trophy!" Honestly, that's what turned him on.

- **A private parking place.** At the beginning of each month, the top sales producer always gets an aptly designated reserved parking space, right near the office front door. Absolutely no one else is allowed to use that parking spot. Trivial? Hardly! It is amazing how much prestige a prime private parking space gives a sales consultant.

- **A photograph.** Each month's top sale consultant also has his or her picture displayed on the wall in the office lobby. Prominently, too: It's a can't-miss 12-inch-by-14-inch photo, with the name on a large gold label, so that everyone coming through the door sees who our top producer is. This, too, is a big deal. Many times visitors will ask questions or comment about the recognition we give our sales people.

- **Field trips.** Not a week goes by that don't get out in the field to help my people close sales. One of the biggest weaknesses I see among sales leaders is their trying to lead only from behind a desk. Show your people that you just don't talk a good game. Get out there and let them watch you do your thing! I love going into the field with my consultants. It helps keeps me fresh. I see first-hand the issues and challenges they are dealing with, and gives me a chance to show them how to close sales and get referrals.

- **Text messaging.** Here's another great tool for motivating your troops. I text each of my sales consultants *four or five times* a day. They know that I care enough to keep track of their daily activity. By sending these messages, I can relay what the other sale reps are doing throughout the day, and by sending group messages we all can celebrate every sale. I actually look for reasons to text my team members several times a day.

OK, have I convinced you how strongly I believe in sales? I should have. It's all about sales! Throughout our Certified Security office we posted several large signs that simply read, *"Everyone Sells."* It really is true: Nothing does happen until someone sells something. A highly motivated sales team can be responsible for the success of an entire company.

SIMPLE *fact*

Every organization rises or falls on leadership.

And it all starts with you as the sale manager. You must master your *trade* as the leader. Every organization rises or falls on leadership; I truly believe that, and always have. Therefore, as the sales leader I always made sure I had a positive attitude. No matter how bad the weather was, or what conflicts might be festering in the office, my team always knew I was in control and had a plan.

Several years ago, for example, my sales team had suffered an absolutely horrible weekend. We did not make even one sale. To add to the gloom, the Monday morning weather forecast was calling for several days of rain and cold weather, making it next to impossible to go prospecting. If that weren't enough, there were no sales leads either, not one. I knew I had better come up with something exciting for my sales team right away. So for our Monday morning meeting I made sure the motivational music was blaring. I kicked off the meeting with a few clever jokes. Never once did I mention our not having sold a thing during the weekend, or the rotten weather. Instead, I kicked off a lead-generation contest that would send my sales reps to the telephones. I had scripts ready and the rules printed . . . and pizza ordered for lunch. I made sure everyone was excited and engaged. It turned out to be one of the most exciting few days of

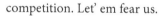

Fearing the competition is for sissies, wimps, whiners and cry babies.

SIMPLE *fact*

the year. As the sales leader, I always had a motivational plan to attack the market with massive amounts of activity. I never complained about how "crummy" things seemed to be going for us. On those dreary days when things were down, my team could count on me to pick things up.

I removed the words *tired, quit* and lose from my vocabulary a long time ago. I also truly believe part of being a strong leader is maintaining a positive, "can-do" attitude. I am obsessed with winning, and with my team winning. I have no desire to maintain an *average* sales force. I expect my sales consultants to be above average. Only winners are allowed to stay on my sales team

Fearing the competition is for sissies, wimps, whiners and cry babies. When one of my sales consultants brings me an ad from one of my competitors, I rarely even acknowledge it. My team is so fired up and motivated that we just outwork the

competition. Let' em fear us.

As I remind my sales team often, we couldn't care less about what the competition is doing. I want competitors worrying about what my highly motivated team is doing. What am I concerned about? The sales presentation my team is preparing and presenting!

A few years ago, at Jacksonville's annual home and patio show, a sales consultant from one of my competitors came over to chat. As we started discussing how great our business was, he observed how there was "enough business out there for everyone. We can all get a nice piece of the pie," he said.

I didn't want a piece of the pie, I replied as respectfully as I could. "I want the whole pie. I want it all." And I wasn't going to be satisfied, I added, until I sold alarm systems and protection to everyone in town.

Now, I know there's no way in the world I could ever convince *everyone* in Jacksonville to become my customers. However, if I work like I really am out to make everyone in Jacksonville my customers, I will get more than my share. Lots more.

If you carry the title *sales manager*, you need to be more than a manager. You must be a leader. You see, there's a big difference between management and leadership. Good managers get things done. They manage things and people. *Leaders* are much different. Not only do leaders get things done, but they also create opportunities, situations and strategies to get done. Leaders are problem solvers. Leaders have people who follow them. If you claim to be a leader and no one is following you, you just might have a problem. If you are a true *sales leader*, you have the ability to improve the performance of the sales team.

I believe anyone can be motivated, at least to some extent. There are no "natural born sales people." Although the individual members of your sales team come from various backgrounds, the sales skills of each members can be improved. And the most important factor in a sales consultant improving his or her sales skills might well be your ability to motivate.

CHAPTER 7

Hold Your Sales Team Accountable

No excuses. Blaming is draining. Explaining is draining. We don't have enough inner plumbing for all that draining.

IT'S LONG BEEN a fundamental of leadership: *"That which is watched grows."*

It's why I'll assert this once again: the two most important components of sales leadership are *motivation* and *accountability*. Without these two, you will never reach your potential as a sales leader. Holding sales people accountable for their activity and their results is critical to the success of your company, and to your sales reps' respective careers. Moreover, when done correctly, your people will appreciate and respect it.

People generally do want to be held accountable for how they pursue their goals and for meeting their responsibilities. They appreciate knowing when they are doing well and when they need to adjust—i.e. improve—their activity at work.

The 15 minutes I once I took to confer with one of my sales consultants remains a vivid encounter. Mark was a new member of my team and he was generating sales quickly. In fact, Mark was on track to achieve a bonus after his very first month; in my office that's a big deal. Despite this early success, Mark still was spending too much time with prospects who I could see were never going to do business with us. Our business model requires every sales consultant to see at least 20 prospects a day; Mark was only seeing about 10 or so per day. He was sort of doing his own thing. During our conversation, I reminded him of

Sales people who complain about being over managed are usually the ones who need it the most.

SIMPLE *fact*

our 20-prospects/day requirement, then stressed how his spending less time with people clearly not interested in ever buying would give him far more time to see people who might well buy. Mark took my advice to heart. As we concluded, he readily agreed to "work smarter" and spend less time with prospects who had very little interest in our products.

Had I ignored this situation and allowed Mark to continue, I eventually would have lost him, and also lost my own credibility as his leader. I had to call him in and hold him accountable. Mark made the proper adjustment in sizing up prospects and managing his time on calls, and is now doing much better.

Would that all sales people respond as Mark did. Not all do, of course. A standard complaint of those who resist being held accountable is, "I'm being micromanaged." It's typically voiced by the millennial generation, but I also hear it from a few veteran sales people not long after they join my team. The irony is, most often these are the individuals who need the most accountability. Left alone, they are not strong enough to manage themselves. In turn, they will never produce the results I require.

As I visit various companies during my "VIP Days" consulting assignments, I see too many managers who are downright afraid to hold their people accountable. They fear possible confrontations, or losing a sales person if they try to enforce the sales guidelines that have been established. Among some is also that fear being labeled a 'Micromanager'. These managers also exhibit a common denominator: *frustration*, and a willingness to put up with mediocrity rather than risk making waves with their employees.

A perfect example of this attitude took place a few months ago when I was meeting with a company's district manager. He was complaining that sales in a few of his offices had been way off target, and one of his younger managers was not getting the job done. In offering more details about this particular manager, he told me he was not holding sales meetings. And he was not completing his required reports. And he was not going out in the field with his sales people at all. What I heard prompted a straightforward question:

"Why are you allowing him to get by with this lack of production?" I asked.

Before the district manager could answer, I quickly offered a suggestion: as soon as possible, meet with his problem child for a performance evaluation, and put him on some sort of action plan. In truth, my long-standing attitude toward this type of behavior is to either change your people . . . or change your people. The district manager's reply was one I hear all too often: You can't treat "millennials" like that, he moaned. They'll quit.

What I was hearing is a classic example of the tail wagging the dog, and it was ever so tempting to snap, "*Let 'em* quit!"

Holding your sales people accountable is a risk well worth taking. To be a good leader, you absolutely must hold your people accountable for their sales activities and performances. Remember: *They* work for *you*.

Ralph, the sales consultant I introduced you to in Chapter 3, is a case in point here, too. Yes, he had solid years of business-to-business selling, and quickly became a top producer after joining us. But he still needed to be held accountable. Unfortunately, Ralph didn't want to be held accountable, and continually pushed back. He soon developed a prima donna attitude, groused about our competitors being better and became confrontational—not only with me but also with virtually everyone in the office. As I explained, I wound up giving him the phone number of a competitor and urged him to call . . . as I was showing him the door. I wasn't about to let Ralph's success hold me hostage.

Accountability is necessary at all levels. And, yes, that includes a company president or owner of the company; they have commitments to meet, just like everyone else. For some, holding their staffs accountable can become an onerous burden. I have seen some so-called "leaders" plead or whine to their staffs to try to get the desired results. I have seen others yell, or act passive-aggressively, or even throw up their hands in frustration. At times, such frustration explodes into outbursts punctuated by foul language. There's no excuse for that, ever. When you get angry and resort to cussing, you are telling everyone you are out of control. It almost always reduces performance and erodes motivation. This is *not* sales leadership, and certainly not the way to hold anyone accountable for anything.

Managers need to be proactive, and face head on whatever conflicts arise. When an employee does not deliver the results you are looking for, deal with the issue immediately! By letting it go, you are sending a message: *It's OK if you break my rules*. You're also saying the commitments the employee agreed to are not really that important. Avoiding a tough situation will usually make that situation worse and more difficult to correct. By dealing with problem right away you are also sending a different message, and one your entire staff will grasp: *I am not afraid to enforce the requirements for our sales position*.

Here are a few of the ways I hold my sales team accountable:

- **Agree on the job description.** During the second interview of my hiring process, I hand prospective sales persons a copy of the sales job description. It is a simple statement and very specific: it lists all of the sales person's responsibilities, describes how my sales people are to dress every day, and enumerates all of our production requirements. At the bottom of the page, sales consultants are to sign the statement, affirming their complete understanding of and commitment to what is required.

Having consultants sign this form is important, and is part of my responsibility as a sales manager. It would be unfair for me to hold someone accountable without my being clear about what is expected, and that I will enforce our requirements.

Once you have established guidelines and responsibilities for your sales team, stick with those rules! Don't keep changing them. It will only cause confusion.

- **Ensure the expectations are reasonable**. My expectations may be considered unduly high for average people. Then again, I am not trying to hire or work with average people. I insist on surrounding myself with overachievers. That said, I do understand that many people I hired over the years never really had to work hard or be held accountable for their work. So I remind everyone who works for me that I am not average and I expect them to be above average.

  The expectations I give my team include: their working eight to 10 hours per day, so they can earn really good money; not only talking a good game but actually delivering a good game; always being honest, and always making an effort. I also remind my team of the two things I will never tolerate from any employee: lying and laziness.

- **Provide the knowledge and tools to meet the expectations.** As their leader, it is my responsibility to make sure they are well trained. All members of my team complete a four-day training class that I personally instruct. I make sure that before they are ever allowed to go on a sales call they know what to say and do.

  Each morning during our sales meeting I provide more training. I want to make sure my team is the best equipped in the industry. It should never fear the competition.

- **Internalize their responsibilities.** In order for sales persons to totally buy-in to their commitment, they must internalize it. They must see their jobs as something bigger than just working eight hours a day five days a week. I want my consultants to see their position as a *career*, not just a *job*. It is up to me to keep them focused on their work.

- **Closely monitor their work.** I work very closely with my sales team. Each morning during the sales meeting, they are required to give me: 1) an account of their activity from the preceding day, and 2) their goals for that day. After the meeting, I simply list their activity for the day on a schedule, so I can check on their accomplishments throughout the day.

I also require my consultants to call me from every sales appointment. They may tell me the prospect was not there for the appointment, or to let me know the prospect has decided to postpone making a positive buying decision. I am not micro managing here. Rather, these calls give me a chance to help my consultant close a sale before departing. I can usually close about on about one-third of these calls. There's one more reason for a sales rep to call: to set the date for our installing protection.

As their manager, I must be available whenever my reps are on sales calls. It's not at all unusual for me to quietly leave my church sanctuary on a Sunday morning and slip into the lobby to take a call from one of my consultants trying to close a sale. They all understand I am there to support them "24/7," and am only a phone call away.

- **Update the sales room scoreboard.** As the chapter on sales meetings explained, every sales room must have a scoreboard. It's where each person's production is there for everyone in the office to see. Rarely does a day go by without other managers in my office stopping at the sales room to see how various members of my team are producing. The scoreboard reveals it all: who's soaring, who's struggling . . . the good, the bad, and the ugly. It delivers a crisp, clear picture of everyone's achievement.

- **Evaluate performances monthly.** This is critical. Your sales people need to know how they are doing. Are you pleased with their overall performance? Say so. If you're not pleased, your team members need to know that right away, too. I meet with each member of my sales team during the first week of each month. Not only is it a great way to hold them accountable but it also enables me to speak directly with each team member. At these one-on-one meetings, we discuss their respective goals and commitments, and I point out any areas where additional training might be required.

- **Make sure they have a clear understanding of the consequences.** If your sales team is doing well and reaching its goals, there is cause for celebration. I remind my team often about the numerous opportunities for advancement within our company, and within the security and alarm industry, and how there's room at the top of our chain of command for any individual who continually succeeds.

If, on the other hand, team members are struggling, they need a prompt and pointed reminder that quick improvement is essential, and that poor performance won't be tolerated. My team understands exactly what is expected of it at all times, and that I will not hesitate to remove someone who is not a good fit.

SIMPLE
fact

> Successful sales leaders understand that they must hold their sales consultants accountable, for their activity, and at the same time keep them motivated.

Holding your sales people accountable for their actions is no stroll in the park, but it is a skill that you can learn. It delivers handsome benefits, too: such as building trust, and getting more things done. Most important, your sales colleagues will respect you more because of it . . . because they know they can count on you. If you're forced out of your comfort zone along the way, that's OK, too. Your managerial and sales leadership capabilities will be stronger as a result.

As the saying goes, "If you want to accomplish great things in your life, surround yourself with successful people." Holding them accountable is what helps mold successful individuals.

A Template for Tough Meetings

Invariably, holding people accountable includes having to deliver bad news and occasionally dealing with confrontation. That, in turn, requires time and preparation. Before dealing with likely confrontation, plan ahead. Think first about what you want the meeting to achieve. Here is a simple formula for having a successful corrective one-on-one session with an employee we'll call Frank.

1. **Plan ahead:** What do you want the result of this meeting to be? Are you hoping Frank will resign, or do you want Frank to improve and stay with the company?

2. **Meet in private:** The meeting really should be "one-on-one," unless you need a human resources staff member to witness a corrective action.

3. **Begin with a compliment:** If your goal is to motivate, and get Frank back on track, always start by reminding him of his contributions to the company, his experience and years of service, or specific skills sets that are valuable to the team.

4. **Deal with the issue:** Hit the issue head on—and without negative emotion. Professional leaders do not get emotional when dealing with an employee. Be very clear and detailed when discussing whatever the problem or short-coming is.

5. Here it is very important to avoid using the words *but* or *however*: Telling Frank how valuable he has been to the company, and then saying, "*but* we have a problem we need to address," is tantamount to admitting, "All that stuff I just you told about how valuable you are is not really true or important."

6. **Have the employee agree:** Once you have explained the issue in detail, be sure to ask Frank for a commitment that the problem will not come up again.

7. **Finish on a positive:** At this point, remind Frank how much you appreciate him, and that you are confident you two will never have this conversation again.

8. **Document, document, document!** Write up a simple document stating the agreement that Frank just committed to. It doesn't have to be complicated. It is a good idea to cite consequences that would result if Frank does not deliver on his promise. Be sure the document is dated and has both your signature and Frank's.

Residential & Small Business Security Consultants Job Description

- Represent yourself and the company in a professional, courteous and responsible manner at all times.

- Attend all scheduled daily sales meeting at 9:00 am unless you have permission from your sales manager.

- Turn in all paperwork by 8:45 am for the previous days' activities.

- Follow the company method of the sales presentation on all sales appointments (iPad presentation, walk through, keypad demo, etc.).

- Contact your sales manager after, or during every appointment with the results: sale, DNS, no shows, cancels.

- Do not reschedule any company appointments on your own. The sales manager or call center manager must be involved.

- "Dress for success" which is defined as long sleeve dress shirt or company provide pullover shirt. Long sleeve dress shirt and tie is recommended. Pressed slacks and shoes that will hold a shine. No docker type slacks. No Polo type shirts, unless they have the company logo on them.. Ladies should wear business attire or a company shirt.

- Use the referral program on every sale.

- Sell at least 5 self-generated approved sales per month.

- Maintain a minimum total of 15 approved sales per month.

- Keep some sort of day planner such as a day timer or electronic organizer.

Date: _____

X_____

Sales Consultant

X_____

Sales Manager

CHAPTER 8

Raising the Bar

Whatever you have going on today, take it up a notch! Tighten up! Get on your game and make a difference. Don't put off doing the hard task! Do it now before you go to lunch.

IF YOU THINK *you have arrived at a certain level of achievement, you need to know that there is someone out there who is doing better than you. There is someone who is playing on a higher level. If you think that you have reached the summit of your success, then you are on your way down. Never be content with where you are. There is another level out there that you might know nothing about. To get there, you just have to take it up a notch. Get more excited. Read more, and don't get trapped in the whirlwind of daily activities. Set time aside ever day to be proactive.*

I jotted down this thought a few years ago, and I still refer to it often. This sort of helps me stay focused on my career and helps me with my priorities. Whenever I think I am doing well (usually because all my friends are telling me so), I think about the words that opened this chapter. I know there is another level of achievement that I can reach if I just keep digging around and never give up.

> There are no natural born leaders. Leadership is developed by keeping a positive attitude, taking risks, and asking yourself; "Why not me."

SIMPLE *fact*

I was very fortunate to be raised in a Christian home that was full of love and laughter. Although we never had a lot of money, we were rich in other ways. My dad was the associate pastor of one of the largest churches in the country, back in the 1950s and 60s. My father had a "can do" attitude about everything he did. When he became the associate pastor of the church, it was very small with only a small handful of members. Under the leadership of both my father and the lead pastor, who was an outstanding preacher, their small church exploded; its Sunday School grew to become the largest in the Southeast.

My father was at the same time very strict with me but also very liberal. When I was in seventh and eighth grades, I remember my dad once posing this challenge: if I could score 100 on my Friday spelling test, *the following week* I could skip school and go fishing with him. That sounds crazy, but it worked. Instead of just skating by and barely scoring a passing grade on my test, I would "nail" it every time with a perfect score.

SIMPLE *fact* | Think BIG and Work Hard! | I was also held accountable when I messed up. There were no excuses for my mistakes with my parents. "If I did the crime, I paid

the time." When I was 16 years old I had bought my own car with money I made mowing lawns and bagging groceries. It was my car and I was very proud. But house rules remained: My parents made sure that I understood I had a curfew. I had to be in the house every night by 11 p.m. No excuses. Well, one night I arrived home at 11:11. I was held up by one of Jacksonville's downtown drawbridges. When I walked in the house, dad had his hand out for the keys to my beloved car. He then placed the keys on top of the television in our living room. They stayed there for two weeks.

Watching my father lead hundreds of volunteer workers by both holding them accountable and motivating them at the same time was a priceless education in leadership. My dad was straightforward: He simply would convince people to take on a task, then hold them accountable for completing it. He also found reasons to praise everyone for a job well done.

I learned a great deal about leadership from my father, more than I can ever recount. Ever since, I've tried to use what I learned to get the best out of those who report to me.

Please understand that I am not special. I am, however, obsessed with success. I have an average IQ, but I also have an incredibly positive attitude. I do not believe there are natural- born leaders. Rather, leadership is an acquired skill. You can become a great leader if you just keep an open mind and are willing to work and learn.

Plenty has been written about the power of a positive attitude. Well, I can tell you that looking on the happy side of life makes you more attractive. No one wants to hang out with or follow a grump. I can put a positive spin on just about any situation. Having a positive attitude is attractive, and it's contagious, too.

When the director of my Sunday School class asked my wife and I to assume a leadership position in helping him direct the class, we readily agreed. We also told him that we could build the class. At that time, it was averaging about 75 to 80 senior adults each Sunday. The director gave us the green light, and within a few months we were averaging more than 120 each Sunday. On two occasions, attendance soared above 300.

How'd we do it? In part because my wife, Judy, assigned more than 30 people to be group leaders, while I went to work motivating the class each Sunday. In less than a year we had more than 60 people responsible for some kind of class task or activity each week. I had become obsessed with building a great class and reaching more people. If I cannot get obsessed with a project or responsibility, then I will not get involved at all.

I am going to give you three guidelines for improving your leadership skills.

1. ADJUST YOUR THINKING TO A HIGHER LEVEL

When Judy and I assumed responsibility for building the class at church, my very first question was: "Where are we going to seat all the new people that we are going to bring in?" You see, I was already thinking at a higher level. Within a few months we had our class room packed every Sunday. And I mean packed, too. About 20 men usually had to stand in the back of the room during the entire hour.

Most people think on an average level. I always think on a higher level. I am not suggesting that I am better than anyone else, but I am always thinking, "Why *not* me?" . . . "Why *not* my sales team?" I believe that success is a choice. I can choose to read a few chapters of a self-help book or I can watch television (a total waste of time).

No one is going to give you a great life or hand you a magic pill that is going to make you a strong sales leader. It's as if some people think that they are going to be sitting around their home one day and there will be a knock at the door. When they open the door, someone will be there with a big box and say, *"Here is an extraordinary life for you!"* Or, *"Here, you are now a great leader. Congratulations!"*

I have news for you. There ain't no one comin' with a big box.

The good news is, you *can* develop and improve your ability to lead. It all starts with your thinking and your attitude. It is an attitude that motivates you to continually put forth maximum effort to raise the bar. Start thinking big. If your sales team is averaging 10 sales per person, why not think of them averaging 20 sales per person? It all starts with what you think is possible. Is it actually possible that you could double your production? Why not? What is stopping you? Dream big and work hard.

In order to get to the next level of success, you must change your way of thinking. Your thoughts and actions are why you are where you are right now. Successful people are obsessed with *what's next*.

SIMPLE *fact*

> If your past ever becomes more important than your future, you are going the wrong way.

I once resigned from a company because it was satisfied with mediocrity. You see, when you quit winning, you just plain quit. I saw people around me who just wanted to get by. I wasn't satisfied, even though I was being paid well at the time. When some of my colleagues in upper management suggested, "Just "keep my head down and run with the herd," I told them, "I don't want to run with the herd, because the herd is not going anywhere."

It is built within us to want more. I think the word *more* might be the most important word in all of nature. Everything that lives wants more and will do just about anything to get more. We want more friends . . . more money . . . more success . . . more love . . . more food . . . more houses . . . more cars . . . and more sales. If you do not have the desire to want *more*, and the desire to grow and to build, then you are dying.

It is mighty important to understand this: if your past achievements are more important to you than your goals and your future, you are in big trouble.

Have the mindset that you will win every time. Why only be a good sales manager when you can be a great sales leader? Why not make your team grow and generate more sales and more sales dollars? It all starts with what level you think on.

"You are who you are and where you are because of what has gone into your mind. You can change who you are and where you are by changing what goes into your mind."—Zig Ziglar

2. OPERATE AT A HIGHER LEVEL

Werner Von Braun, who headed NASA's Space Research and Development for the Apollo IV Project in the 1960s, once offered a short but thought-provoking statement about the Saturn V rocket, which propelled the spacecraft for that mission: "The Saturn V has 5,600,000 parts."

Can you imagine trying to put that thing together? Even if it had a 99.9% reliability, there would still be 5,600 defective parts. Yet, the Apollo IV mission flew a textbook flight with only two anomalies occurring; it demonstrated a reliability of 99.999%! If the average automobile with 13,000 parts were equally reliable, it would have its first defective part after about . . . 100 years; my wife's car just had its second recall, and it's only 2 years old.

What's the difference? NASA holds itself to a higher level of performance than the automotive industry. We need to hold ourselves to higher levels of performance.

Most people are average. They operate at an average level of everything—which is why they are just average. The difference between average and extraordinary is not that difficult.

Sometimes I think to myself: "I can't believe I get all this recognition because I really don't consider what I do as necessarily extraordinary." But, I keep winning awards, getting asked to speak, getting interviewed on TV. People pay to come and hear me speak at my Proven Sales Strategies seminars. I get asked to write for our trade magazines. This stuff is not that hard. I just devote massive action to everything I do.

> When average people or companies compete with people or companies of extraordinary action, the average will usually fail.

SIMPLE *fact*

I came into the alarm industry in 1986 with no idea about whether 25 sales a month was a good performance or a bad one. No one told me that 50 sales was a good month. I just figured that there are about 10 to 12 hours a day to work, six days a week—so sell two or three systems a day and life would be good. I sold 3,500 in six years and 90% of my sales were self-generated. I did not want a company lead; those people might just be shopping. Working at a higher level than anyone else in the company was an obsession for me. I was doing what others in my industry considered to be massive action.

Not to me. We are born to move at a massive level. If you have a 4- or 5-year-old, you know what I mean. Just watch my 6-year-old grandson. Caleb never slows down. He runs everywhere. Everything he does is at a massive level. I guess somewhere as we matured, we decided that we needed to take it easy.

One of my biggest fears in life is to be considered average, or for my children or grandchildren to be considered average. I am proud to say my three children are far from average. They strive to overachieve at everything. Judy and I have eight grandchildren, five of whom are millennials. These young people are far from average. They know how to work and all are very successful.

When average people or companies compete with people or companies of extraordinary action, the average will usually fail. There might be a company out there you compete with that is extraordinary. If you're not just as extraordinary, it's a competition you will lose. As a sales person, if your competitor is better prepared and more knowledgeable than you are, when you go head to head you likely will lose the sale.

To me, average is tantamount to a terminal disease. It puts me to sleep. Average to me means you are doing just enough to get by. Average anything will not get you an extraordinary life.

SIMPLE *fact* | If you are the smartest person in your circle of friends, you need more friends.

I asked a friend of mine, a pastor in central Florida, how his church was doing. "We are holding our own," was his reply. "Holding your own what?" I quickly asked. "Get to work and build a church!"

I surround myself with above-average people. At least once every week I go to lunch with above average people. I call them my inner circle. None of these men are in my industry. Rather, they're each overachievers in their respective industries. After each lunch meeting, I never fail to walk away with something I can apply to my life.

When my sales people go on a sales call, it better not be average. It has to be extraordinary. I want our prospects to be dazzled by our presentations. I also don't want my sales people earning average paychecks. I want them to be the highest paid in the alarm industry. With a team of brand new sales people, we have a closing rate of 82% on the first call.

Success demands continuous attention. Don't ever slow down, don't ever take a break, and don't ever listen to others who tell you to slow down. It does not matter to them whether you win or lose. But it matters plenty to you.

3. DON'T JUST COMPETE—DOMINATE!

I really couldn't care less about my competition. I find it interesting—and badly misguided—that so many sales organizations develop a business model based on what *the competition* is doing. My program was built on my ability to train and motivate excellent sales people. I am more concerned about my sales team than any competitor's. As I see it, I don't lose sales to my competition. If we do lose a sale, it was because my sales person did not do his or her job correctly. People buy from individuals, not companies. A lot of companies believe they must have the industry's lowest price to win the sale. Baloney! The reason they are the cheapest is because they suck at sales. If they had to rely on the professionalism of their sales team, they wouldn't stand a chance.

I do not worry about keeping up with anyone. I want everyone to worry about keeping up with me. When a sales rep brings me a competitor's advertising piece,

I just say, "OK. So what?" I do not want to compete with anyone. Total domination is what I'm after. I don't want my little piece of the pie. Give me the whole pie.

To dominate, you simply must do what your competition will not or cannot do. I *want* an unfair advantage; every chance I can get.

A few months ago I ran into the sales manager of my biggest competitor. He candidly told me that when his sales team comes up against my team on a call, it knows it cannot win the sale, even though its prices are lower than ours. He said we have an unfair advantage. The *unfair* advantage he was referring to is simply the fact that we just plain outwork his guys. We dominate the competition.

During my years as the sales manager at Certified Security, I once received a call from a doctor who lived about 50 miles from our office. He told me he was interested in getting a security system for the home he had just purchased. I immediately asked if we could come out to visit him at his new home. He had a very hectic schedule, he replied, and the only time he was available would be the following Saturday at 7 a.m. He also told me that he had already had met with one of my competitors, and that two other companies he had called told him they couldn't come out that early on a Saturday.

> To dominate your market, you simply must do what your competition will not or cannot do.

SIMPLE *fact*

"We will have no problem meeting with you at 7 on Saturday morning," I assured him.

When we arrived—at exactly 7 a.m.—he was pleasantly surprised. He even invited us to join him and his wife for breakfast. We spent about two hours with the doctor and his wife that morning and made a really nice sale. As we were walking out the front door and saying, "Thank you," he stopped. Then he told us our price was a little higher than our competitor's, but he had selected our company anyway. He liked us better, he said. Besides, we had actually arrived on time for the appointment, just as we had promised.

Don't play by the preconceived rules. Don't get sucked into believing you have to run your business by some predetermined set of achievement levels. Never judge yourself by comparing yourself to someone else.

Say your industry has an unwritten standard that a sales person should make at least 10 sales per month. Who says 10 is good or bad? Just because that's average doesn't mean it's good. Take it to the next level. Raise the bar and demand 20 sales a month. Hey, that's still not even one sale a day.

Your attitude needs to be, "I am the dominator. I *will* win the sale. I am *not* going away. I *own* this space." I coached a winning high school girls basketball team for several years. I taught my forwards that they owned the space inside the paint. If anyone dared to venture into their space, there was going to be some drama.

Competition? I repeat: Competition is for sissies, wimps, whiners and cry babies. Domination is what you want. Don't get caught up trying to imitate the actions of your competition. You want them to be following you. I love it when my competition is always trying to figure out what we are up to.

Build success that's so great everyone wants to be part of it; when you are over-achieving and your sales people are on their "A Game." You will attract a lot of sales people who will want to join your team. I once had the most experienced sales consultant in Jacksonville contact me about working for me. In fact, the last five sales people I hired each sought me out. I did not have to run an ad anywhere.

It is very likely that your company has great products, attractive pricing, a fine reputation, appealing brochures, and wonderful training and support. In the final analysis, though, none of this stuff really matters. None of it has any value at all if there is not a corps of strong, professional sales people to tell the story. And it all starts with you, the sales leader.

All you gotta do is what they won't do

To get the *unfair advantage* over your competition, simply do the things your competition won't or cannot do! Here are just a few things you can do to create that unfair advantage:

- Make sure you have a live, smiling face answering your phones. I refer to our receptionist as the Director of First Impressions;
- Only hire the best sales people to represent your company;
- Provide excellent training for your sales people;
- Sell a product that has name brand recognition:
- Do massive amounts of work:
- Make sure your image is impressive. The appearances of your company vehicles, sales people and technicians are very important;
- Get involved in every community event you can;
- Write articles for your local papers;
- Your competition is apt to show up late for sales calls because it's considered acceptable. It's not! Show up on time; never ever be late for a sales call.

- Break the rules: People don't think they can conduct business on Sunday. Sunday evening was my best time to call my referrals.

- Text the new customer a selfie "thank you" video after each sale. Your competitors cannot figure that out. They're too lazy.

CHAPTER 9

Training and Coaching

SOMEWHERE TODAY PEOPLE are learning new sales skills. If you are not learning, when you compete with them you will lose.

Over the years I've had the privilege of observing and conferring with scores of sales teams. The common denominator among many of them was their failure to hit their sales goals. There were myriad reasons for their missing the mark. But when I dug in and began asking questions about their sales production, two reasons repeatedly appeared: quotas that had been set too high, and too few sales people on board to even come close to reaching the target quota. In digging still deeper, I too often found a glaring weakness: *lack of training*. In fact, fewer than 35% of the companies I visit have a specific sales training program. The consequences are predictable. No organized training program begets low closing percentages and/or too few appointments . . . which frequently begets a third consequence: poor attitudes infecting the sales team.

When we founded Certified Security Systems many years ago, one of our first tasks was developing a very specific sales training program. I first determined the topics that needed to be part of our training agenda, then developed outlines, PowerPoint slides and workbooks. Within a few weeks, we had in place a first-class training program that every sales consultant attended. It insured that each sales representative completely understood our product and sales process.

> You must have a sales training program, period! No excuses.

SIMPLE *fact*

You *must* have a sales training program, period! No excuses. Your sales team will never reach its potential if you do not first take the time to make sure everyone on your team is well trained in all of their respective areas of responsibility.

SIMPLE *fact*

> Training requires interactive participation between the trainer and the trainee.

While critical for each and every sales person, training alone will not get the job done. There also must be continual coaching to complement the training, once the initial instruction concludes. First, though, let's focus on the training itself.

Most sales managers I have met think that they are really good trainers. I guess we all like to hear ourselves talk. However, training is much more than simply presenting volumes of information. I long ago lost count of the "training classes" I endured that were a total waste of time. I could have gotten the same information and motivation from a book. If you're responsible for training your sales people, you'd first better consider carefully how you are going to go about the task. What skill sets do you need to be the excellent trainer you envision yourself being? What classes do *you* need to attend? What books do you need to read to develop your skills?

I have been training both sales people and sales leaders for more than 25 years. When I first took on the responsibility as a corporate trainer, I was given the job solely because I could sell, not because I was a good trainer. It didn't take me long to realize I had plenty to learn about sales training. I was only telling my trainees how I did it. I explained how I prospected, and the techniques I used to close sales. It didn't work. Many of those who completed my early classes were not successful—because I had been trying to persuade them to just do what I did. I assumed everyone had the same sales talent I had.

Well, not everyone did, notwithstanding their capabilities, attitudes and ambitions. To make my training more practical, I realized I had to base my teaching and training on the personalities of my trainees.

There is much more to training than just giving out a lot of information. There is a huge difference between *training* and *education*. Training requires interactive participation between the trainer and the trainee. Education is someone conveying information. You must be smart enough to watch and learn from more experienced and better trainers. To this day, whenever I attend another training class as a

> I define on-the-job training this way: "riding with someone else and picking up his or her bad habits."

SIMPLE *fact*

trainee, I carefully watch and note the various techniques the trainer uses to hold everyone's attention for hours at a time. I've learned a great deal about the different ways of testing my trainees, to ensure all the information is understood and absorbed.

Several sales groups I have met rely on video for their training. It saves the sales manager time and allows trainees to work at their own individual paces. Many videos are professionally produced and feature excellent content. If you are going to provide video training, keep in mind that the best training for sales people is always interactive. It allows the trainees to ask the trainer questions, and that's a key component. A second key component of video sales training is having the trainer serve as a facilitator: introducing various topics and being available to respond to questions.

Whatever kind of organized training you provide, it is important to understand a few basic fundamentals:

- **On-the-job training doesn't work.** I define on-the-job training this way: "riding with someone else and picking up his or her bad habits." After my new consultants complete my four-day class, I have no problem having them individually ride along on a sales call with one of my veterans, but they need to understand they are likely so see or hear things that might be contrary to what they were taught. I would never entrust one of my existing sales reps with the responsibility of training a new employee in the field.

- **All new sales people must complete a classroom training program.** No matter how glowing the backgrounds of your new hires may be, it still is essential for all of them to complete your training class. Please do not assume that, just because a Mark or a Marcia has solid industry experience, either is qualified to start selling your product. Not so!

- **Start and stop on time.** If you start your classes late, you are likely sending a message to your new employee that you are somewhat disorganized. Moreover, you're telling them it's OK to be late. Keep your promise to start —and stop—on time.

- **Keep the room bright.** This is a pet peeve of mine. I'm apt to be standing in front of these trainees for about 7 hours a day. I need to hold their attention. Experience tells me that if the room is bright and exciting they'll be more likely to stay engaged.

- **Use humor.** If you lack a sense of humor, get someone else to do the training for you. Lighten up and make the class enjoyable. If you are boring, you will fail as a trainer.

- **No interruptions.** Make sure to have someone else on your staff handle your other responsibilities during training sessions. When I served as sales manager and sales trainer at Certified Security, I made sure the general manager was on hand to handle any calls that came in for me during class time. If you are consistently interrupted while training, you cannot possibly stay on track. Your trainees will be sitting there with nothing to do while you are handling phone calls. That's downright rude.

- **Give 'em a break.** I always announce early on the approximate times we'll take breaks. My rule of thumb is trainees need a break at least every 90 minutes.

- **Test them throughout the day.** Testing helps determine if your trainees are learning. It also delivers other benefits. If they understand they will be tested throughout the day, they are more likely to pay attention.

Testing is a wonderful training tool. All of my **written tests** are multiple choice quizzes. After they're completed, I have the trainees exchange papers. I then go around the room and have them give the correct answers to the various questions. This tactic gives us a chance to discuss in much more detail topics related to the questions.

In addition to written quizzes, there are other methods of testing your trainees. Each morning I take time **to review** some of the important topics from the preceding day by calling on people in the class. This, too, always turns out to be a valuable learning experience. Later during the day I will also **ask questions** about what we discussed earlier in that session.

SIMPLE *fact*

As the sales leader, it's your responsibility to continually watch them very carefully, and to make sure no one is dropping the ball.

Never assume that just because you are spewing out a lot of information your trainees understand it all, and are ready to apply your wisdom. This is why it is so important to set aside time to make sure each sales person "gets it," has the proper tools to be successful, and will be able to wield them. Without proper sales training, your team will not reach its potential.

Coaching

In professional sports, training usually begins before the season starts. It's when teams begin playing that coaching becomes so important, right from the first moments of the opening game. Waiting until halftime to make adjustments, New England Patriots coach Bill Belichick once said crisply in response to a question, "is too late!"

The same can be said of sales training and coaching. Everyone must undergo training, but when the training is completed the coaching begins and continues. Never assume that a well-trained sales person in the field can handle every possible situation that might arise—or *erupt*. Now that your team members have completed your training class, the focus shifts to ensuring what they were taught is being applied. As the sales leader, it's your responsibility to continually watch them very carefully, and to make sure no one is dropping the ball. Are your representatives following your sales presentation guidelines? Are they prospecting every day? Do they need help in overcoming objections? With closing a sale? Are they hitting their sales quotas?

Consistent coaching is as essential as thorough training. Without it, most sales people will develop habits that keep them from reaching their full potential. Yes, they might be generating acceptable sales level, but you still probably could coach them up to the next level of achievement. And that's what you should strive for.

It is your job as the sale leader and coach to stay on top of the-day to-day activity of your sales team. Every day.

Essentials

In setting up any sales training program, there are certain topics that must be included in your curriculum:

- Company policies and procedures;
- Fundamentals of sales that apply directly to your industry;
- Product training;
- The various steps of your sales presentation;
- Closing the sale and overcoming objections;
- Lead generation.

Obviously, it will take several days to adequately train on these topics. But it will be time well-spent.

CHAPTER 10

Practical Goal Setting

If you do not step forward, you always will be in the same place.

FIRST, A DISCLOSURE: I second guessed myself about including this chapter. Volumes already have been written about setting goals, including scores of worthwhile ideas by some of the best sales trainers in the country.

Even so, any book about sales leadership had better include goal-setting. Omitting the topic would be a glaring omission, for

You cannot think and plan without setting goals.

SIMPLE *fact*

it's part and parcel to a sales leader's responsibilities. Any sales leader worth his salt is obsessed with growth, continually planning for the future and continually thinking about "What's next?" You cannot think and plan without setting goals.

I am going to focus on what I describe as fairly short-term goals, rather than the month-to-month quotas that managers typically focus on. After all, if you hit all your short term goals you also will nail the big ones.

I set goals for myself every day—and you can't get more short-term than that. It has become a way of life for me. Every day, without fail, I write down what I want to accomplish by the time the sun has set. As you might suspect, I'm also one of those characters who makes a list of what I am going to do around the house on weekends. Yes, I can drive the people closest to me a little crazy now and then. But to me it is simple and straightforward, and delivers a great feeling of accomplishment when I have completed the tasks.

A few years ago I penned this notion: "If, at the end of the day, you can honestly say you accomplished all of your written goals, then you can say you had a great day." The notes that I write to myself every day are usually simple short-term goals. Also on the list are several long-range goals that require daily activity.

SIMPLE *fact*

> A pretty good first step would be simply asking yourself: "Where do you see yourself in five years?"

This book is Exhibit A of what I'm taking about. I have friends who the past 10 years or so were telling me I needed to write down all my sales leadership ideas. To me, though, writing a book seemed to be a monumental task. Well, on January 1, 2017, I made the commitment to begin writing. I came up with a 100-day action plan to complete this project. As you can see, I did. It is amazing how simple a huge project becomes when you break it down into bite-size pieces. By simply committing to writing every day for a relatively short period of time, I stayed right on schedule and completed the initial manuscript within my 100-day goal.

Without question, achieving goals and making changes in your life requires taking risks. They can create uncomfortable situations. This is why reaching new goals is such a challenge. But it's also a common challenge. If you are an owner, manager or sales leader, you earned your

> Goals are only for those who want to go somewhere!

SIMPLE *fact*

position in your company because you took a risk. You moved out of your comfort zone and did something to get noticed.

Most people don't set goals. They just deal with whatever they happen to encounter each day. These are usually good people, too, and many appear to be successful. But most of them never reach their full potential. Setting goals doesn't have to be complicated or formal. A pretty good first step would be simply asking yourself: "Where do you see yourself in five years?" Even if it's just "one year," at least you are thinking about the future.

I'll forever be proud of my oldest grandson, Brandon, who was asked by his supervisor if he could he see himself becoming a supervisor within five years. Brandon replied how he could see himself running *the entire company* within five years. Now, that is an extremely lofty goal for a 23-year-old young man, but I love Brandon's attitude. At least he's not afraid to think big.

Why don't people identify and pursue goals? For several reasons. Let's start with **fear**. They're afraid they might fail and they'll feel bad, so why try? Fear appears in many forms: It could be **fear of the unknown**. People just don't know where

SIMPLE *fact*

> By making a note of the problems that might arise, you will better prepare yourself to deal with them.

to start, or what to do. There's also **fear of change**. Those who get stuck in their comfort zone tend to get comfortable, and don't see the need to improve their lives or increase their value to their companies. Others recoil at the **fear of rejection** when thinking about a goal. "What if someone thinks it is silly?" they needlessly ask themselves.

If you are dealing with any of these fears, here are a few ideas to overcome them, and help you get on with setting some goals in your life:

1. *Think big!*—You always must have high hopes.

2. *Start small*—Break your goal down into small bite-size pieces; you will be surprised how much you will accomplish. You might start by getting a library card.

3. *Go with your strengths*—Use whatever you are pretty good at to your advantage.

4. *Do your homework*—Study your target (goal).

5. *Take a risk*—Start by doing something simple, something out of the ordinary, at least for you. How about reading a chapter in a motivational book each evening, or learning a new closing technique? After you complete the task, you will feel good about yourself and will be more likely to continue the activity tomorrow.

6. *Avoid negative people!*—They will drag you down every time. They don't care whether you succeed or fail.

7. *Visualize success*—What will it look like or feel like to hit that goal? Think about how much more you can be if you just stick with it, and keep chasing your goal.

8. *Learn to endure the rough spots*—They're what I call speed bumps on the highway to success. You are going to have some disappointments. Everyone does. Be aware that they are just temporary.

9. *Always have a positive attitude*—Keep telling yourself you can do it. I do it all the time, and am a big believer in "self-talk."

In my opinion, goals are not for everyone—as strange and as contradictory as that may sound. Goals are only for those who want to go somewhere! If you are one of these success-driven individuals, if you do want to become more than you are, here is my seven-step formula for success.

SIMPLE *fact*

How are going to feel knowing you did it? What are you going to learn along the way?

If you will follow these simple, practical steps, you can grow, you can develop into a better leader, you can enjoy more success, and you can become more valuable to your organization.

1. **Identify your goal and be very specific.** When I started building my sales team at Certified Security Systems, I was very careful to set a goal that I clearly understood. Rather than set a goal to build a good sales team, my goal was to have six well-trained sales people on board within four months. With that in mind, I began to carefully select my team.

2. **Set deadlines.** When setting short term or intermediate goals, your time lines should probably be no longer than a few months. When I began building my sales team, I kept the end in mind. I knew the exact date I wanted to accomplish my goal.

3. **Identify the obstacles.** Hey, there are going to be problems. It is not going to go perfect; it never does. Think about what could stop you or slow you down. Be aware of other responsibilities that might interfere with your plan, or any distractions other activity causes that could momentarily stop you; for instance, what if you lose sight of your goal or become frustrated? By making a note of the problems that might arise, you will better prepare yourself to deal with them. You won't be blindsided.

4. **Identify the resources achievement requires.** This is a big one. If you are going to succeed at anything new, you will need help. When I started this book, I really had no idea where to start. Do you start with some kind of introduction? Or just plunge into chapter 1? How many pages should be in the book? What about titles for the various chapters? Who can edit the book, and how do I get it published? The tasks seemed overwhelming, so I immediately made a list of the resources I needed. I made note of the training I might need, and people I needed to interview. I sought out a few successful local writers. I took each of them to lunch several times. Beforehand, I had a list of questions to ask. Their help was invaluable. I was smart enough to know what I didn't know, so I sought out the experts.

5. **Identify the skills and tools achievement requires.** If your goal is to increase your team's sales by 20% next month, you had better determine what tools you need to make that happen: Perhaps a really cool sales contest; or special pricing on your most popular product or service; or a nice commission bonus. You must carefully think about what it is going to take to hit that goal. *"What tools do you need?"*

6. **Develop a plan of action.** OK, now it's time to go to work. You're now ready to put your goal in writing—and it's when you do put it on paper that you transform your wish into your goal. Make a note of your specific goal and establish a time line, then break the time line into small segments. If, say, your goal for your sales team is to have 50 sales next month, make a note on how many sales you need each week, and then each day. Now, carefully track your success (or lack of it). Breaking your goals down into small segments like this allows you to manage more carefully. And, you won't be surprised at the 25th of the month when you only have 30 sales. Before you ever launch your goal, make sure you clearly understand what it's going to take to hit it. How many calls does your team need to make each week and each day to generate those 50 sales? Is additional training needed? Or do you as the manager need to spend time in the field with your sales reps to help ensure success? What tools could you use to motivate your team?

7. **Finally, list the benefits of crushing your goal.** This is the fun part! How are going to feel knowing you did it? What are you going to learn along the way? You actually accomplished something most people will rarely achieve. You set a goal and you hit it. It is time for celebrating your success. . . . I love it when a plan comes together.

My wife Judy and I have reared three very successful children who are now adults. Ever since they were old enough to understand, we have reminded them they are not average and we did not expect average behavior from them. We taught them all to set goals to become better than themselves. Everyone who knows my offspring will readily testify that they all are over achievers. They are not normal or average. We started encouraging them to take behavioral risk at a very early age. We taught them to get out of their comfort zone and speak to everyone. We taught them self-confidence, and that they could become leaders as they over achieved. They understood early on that the difference between just being good (average) or being great is really not that big of a deal. Set a few simple goals for yourself, work hard and you, too, will be perceived as an overachiever—because you will have become one.

There's an interesting thing about achieving goals and moving out of your comfort zone: After a short period of time, what was uncomfortable becomes comfortable. Once upon a time, your team was producing 40 sales a month and it was very comfortable. But after you set some very practical, simple goals and increased your effort, 50 sales became comfortable.

Now you are ready to reach for more.

CHAPTER 11

'Mavericks' On Your Team? Leverage 'Em

PROBLEMS NEVER LEAVE you where they find you. They will make you bitter or better, and the choice is yours.

Count on it: At some point in your career as a sales manager you will collide with someone on your team who's routinely rebellious and very difficult to work with; indeed, an apt description of this colleague might well be "a tried-and-true pain in the neck."

Don't fret. And do not misunderstand what you are about to read.

No member of your team should ever be allowed to openly criticize you as the manager and leader. Tolerating that type of behavior will cost you your credibility in a heartbeat—as it probably should. You see, the leader of a sales team is not always the manager. If you are a ranking sales manager who does not promptly take corrective action with what I call *mavericks,* you will still have your manager's title, but nothing else. It will be the mavericks who effectively become the leaders of your team and undermine your authority each and every day.

> SIMPLE *fact*
>
> If you are a ranking sales manager who does not promptly take corrective action with what I call mavericks, you will still have your manager's title, but nothing else.

Over the years I have had my share of mavericks on my sales teams; maybe more than my share, or so it seemed at the time. One of them was a fellow I'll call Bret.

Before joining my team, Bret had worked for another alarm company in another state for many years. He soon became my top producer, and his success won him the respect of others on our sales team. Bret not only was producing and selling, but also demonstrating his industry knowledge. In turn, I learned early on that I did need to treat Bret just a little differently than my team's other members, but to do so without showing any favoritism. My job as the sales leader was to get the very best from each person on the sales team without compromising my integrity as a leader. Yet as capable as Bret was, he also exhibited a pair of glaring weaknesses: a somewhat rebellious attitude, and a monstrous ego.

I'll forever remember how I responded: Soon after joining us, I asked Bret to come into my office, then quietly closed the door.

"Bret, you're a terrific sales consultant, and everybody knows it, "I began. "I sincerely hope we can work well together and get along, and I will do everything I can to build a great relationship."

Having praised Bret, I then explained, as professionally as I could, that I was the manager and leader of the team, no one else. Next I delivered this word of caution:

"If you ever openly challenge me in front of the sale team," I said, "I will terminate you."

With that, I concluded on another positive note, plus a proposal of sorts: "Bret, I know you are going to be my top producer. And I will be counting on you to help me train and work with some of our new sales consultants. They'll benefit from your skills and experience."

SIMPLE
fact

| He was still a maverick, to be sure. But he was my maverick, and became my right hand man. |

That I am recounting my words should affirm the fine relationship Bret and I developed, and how he worked for me for many years. He was still a maverick, to be sure. But he was *my* maverick, and became my right hand man. Bret was the colleague I could count on to help with the new sales reps, and even cover for me when I was on vacation.

What helped me forge a good relationship with Bret can help you forge solid relationships with your own Bret . . . or Bart or Bill or Bob or Bruce. Here are some tips to keep in mind when dealing with the mavericks you will encounter:

• **Deal with them one-on-one**—Before I ever rolled out a new sales contest or introduced a new product, I would huddle with Bret and my other mavericks to get their buy-in. And when I introduced the contest or new product, I would always include my maverick in the rollout.

• **Work as closely with the maverick as possible**—Often these top producers are "lone wolves." They neither need nor want anyone assisting them on sales calls.

Even so, try to team up with your maverick when possible, if only for one or two sales calls a month. Also solicit your maverick's opinion about some of your ideas to increase sales or attain the new goals you've set.

• **Never show favoritism to this person**—Although your mavericks might be your best at closing sales, be very careful not to ever let them think you are giving them special treatment or favors. Just as important: don't ever let your other sales reps think you are favoring these individuals.

• **Understand that you can mold your maverick into a leadership position**—If you, as the leader, can forge a solid working relationship with mavericks, I believe they can be developed for leadership positions (assuming, of course, they have the requisite skills and interest). Give them some responsibilities and help them develop their leadership skills, then see what unfolds. One of the greatest strengths of a leader is helping others become leaders.

• **Don't be afraid to make the difficult decision**—If a maverick's negative attitude begins to affect the production or attitude of the other sales consultants on your team, do not be afraid to terminate this person. Don't put off the decision, either. Remember my maxim about never letting any sales consultant hold you hostage, no matter what? That applies to mavericks, too.

• **Never get emotional**—When dealing with or confronting a maverick, never lose your cool. Keep a calm demeanor and deal with whatever challenge arises logically.

Your top producer is also apt to be your biggest headache, and potentially your most chronic rule-breaker. *"Because I am bringing in so much business, those rules don't apply to me"* Is how a maverick typically thinks.

> Don't ever let your other sales reps think you are favoring these individuals.

SIMPLE *fact*

Don't for one minute tolerate this mindset; ever. By giving a maverick special treatment, you are sending a message to others on your team that you are showing favoritism, or that you are a weak leader. Set careful guidelines that apply to all the members of your sales team, and stick with them.

Part II

Developing your PPP: "People Persuasive Power"

If you've come this far, you don't need being reminded about why sales champions are sales champions. You already know why: They constantly look for a better way, because being "good enough" . . . never is. Sales champs never are satisfied with the status quo, and continually look for ways to find more prospects and close more sales. They attend seminars regularly. They are forever eager to learn. And, they are voracious readers of books like this one.

So now it's time to pick up your highlighter or note pad, and carefully consider what I'm about to lay on you in these next four chapters. Fear not. I'm not about to subject you to some "wifty" B-school theories or suspicious-sounding hype. What's in store is all grass roots sales stuff: plain and simple techniques that I've used over the years to find and close thousands of sales in the alarm industry, both commercial and residential. They're as effective today as they've ever been.

CHAPTER 12

The Secret Formula

The more you are able to influence people around you, the more you can achieve.

I WOULDN'T EVEN try to guess at the number of ways to define a professional sales consultant. However, I'm not interested in reading or hearing any of them. To me, there's but one no-nonsense, hard-core term that says it all: *"Persuade people to do what you want them to do."*

That's what we sales persons do. In the real world of business and selling, we are *professional persuaders*. The acronym I've coined for this reality is **PPP**. It stands for **People Persuasive Power**.

In one way, shape or form, everyone sells. My wife sells me on where she wants to go out for dinner. When my grandson, Caleb, was a baby, I watched first-hand how he masterfully sold his mother. When his mom would lay him down in the crib, Caleb would start crying, as if there was a diaper pin stuck in his butt. Mom immediately picked him up . . . and Caleb would stop crying. When mom put him back in the crib, Caleb started crying once

> Persuade people to do what you want them to do.

SIMPLE *fact*

again. And mom picked him up once again. Caleb had ably persuaded his mother that he needed to be with her, rather than be alone in his crib. In the blink of an eye, my little grandson had figured out how to make the sale. In time, Caleb's mom began selling, too, in her own way. She persuaded Caleb that sleeping was beneficial—by leaving him alone in his crib. Initially, Caleb was a tough customer, but he came around.

See what I mean when say everyone sells? And because everyone does, I don't buy the old notion of *natural-born* sales people. Now and then I'll glance at birth announcements in our local newspaper. Never once have I read of a woman giving birth to a salesman. On the other hand, I do agree that the environment in which we grew up may have had a direct influence on our persuasive skills. Yet whatever lessons circumstances may impart, I remain firmly convinced that the majority of top sales professionals succeed as they do because they fine-tuned their **People Persuasive Power** over the years. I've seen it over and over. Some folks say I'm a living example myself.

Let's start with my secret formula for success in sales: **CI + PPA = SOP**.

Correct Image + Planned Positive Action = Success on Purpose

Correct Image

Correct image has everything to do with how your prospect feels about you and the company you represent. I think the issue of image is a big deal these days, especially with more and more "professional" businesses adopting "business casual" dress policies. While I have no problem with it per se, I have seen morph out of control.

A year or so ago I visited a company that had taken *business casual* to a whole new level—in the wrong direction. The sales team responsible for meeting both business owners and homeowners were dressed in t-shirts and blue jeans. Their collective appearance was a direct reflection of the leadership. The company's office was a mess, and its service and installations trucks were dirty. The organization's overall image was, in a word, *sloppy*. Given that image, I wouldn't buy a thing from this company.

Compare that image with the one I received at Redwire Security in Tallahassee, Florida, where I once had the privilege of assisting with some training. The image of this firm, in a word, was *incredible*. The Redwire office was very clean and tidy. That alone told me something. Ted Frazee, the president, made sure that every Redwire red truck looked good, and that the sales team appeared sharp. From the receptionist who greeted you to the website to the technician who installs the systems, everything at Redwire appeared to be first class. It still does, too. I wouldn't hesitate to recommend this company, just based on how it appears.

Having the correct image has nothing to do with what *you think* looks good. Rather, it has everything to do with what *your prospect expects* you and your company to look like. When you show up at a prospect's home or business, do you appear to have your act together . . . in the prospect's eyes? Do you appear to be trustworthy? You'd better. Remember, you are asking business owners and homeowners to trust you with the protection of their most valuable assets.

For the sales consultant, correct image means neat and clean appearance. Everything about you—*everything*—should reflect you as being a professional at your trade. If you show up at the customer's location in a beat-up car wearing wrinkled clothes, chances are you won't make the sale, and you might never know why. Correct image also includes having your paperwork in order and having a first-class sales presentation.

Do things during your sales presentation that your competition cannot or will not do.

Throughout these next few chapters I'll be urging you to go that extra mile when dealing with your prospects. Do things during your sales presentation that your competition cannot or will not do. They may seem small, but they're not. They're huge. And No. 1 is demonstrating a first-class image. Remember, *"People buy from individuals, not companies."*

Whether I'm on a commercial or residential sales call, it is essential for me to separate myself from the competition. I want my prospects to understand without a doubt that they are dealing with a polished professional. My goal is to always "dazzle" my prospects with an incredible sales presentation.

You need to *honestly* ask yourself this question: Are you personally demonstrating the image that your prospects expect from someone selling life safety? The answer has to be *yes*. The good news is that these days it's much easier to impress your prospects. It may be as basic as showing up on time and appearing to have your act together. Chances are, some of your competitors won't be so impressive. Just one look from your prospects should be all it takes to distinguish you from and the competition.

Planned Positive Action

Lead-generation activity is a topic I'll devote more attention and detail to in subsequent pages. The point I want to stress here is that you need to have a plan of action every day. A good day-planner is a sales person's best friend. True sales professionals show up for work *every* day with plan of attack. They don't ever sit back and wait for a manager to hand them directives or suggestions about what they should do on a given day. Have a proactive plan to attack your market every day.

Make sure yours is a *positive* plan, too. Certainly, every day carries over issues that you need to clean up from yesterday. That's part of business life. There also might be conference calls or meetings you must attend. That's all well and good. Just make sure that somewhere, somehow you are taking planned positive action every day. Your most valuable asset is your time. Maximize that time by creating new prospects every day.

Success on Purpose

I have found the harder I work the luckier I get. In truth, luck really has nothing to do with it. In just six years I sold about 3,500 alarm systems; believe me, I was not lucky. In earning a handsome income for my family, I worked some mighty long hours. I also did my level best to improve, and comes as close as I could to mastering my sales skills.

My family, in turn, can tell you that during this six years we did not take a family vacation. You might be thinking, *"Well that's not for me. I need my time off."*

Yes, I agree wholeheartedly that you should put your family way before your work. But I also submit that one of the best things you can do for you family is to be successful at work. It's not a question of "either/or," but rather "both/and." For me it was no big deal, because I loved my job and truly looked forward to going to work every day. As crazy as it may sound, my commitment to tackling massive amounts activity and working long hours enabled me to enroll my children in private schools and buy the fastest fishing boat in northeast Florida. My family appreciated it. And, in spite of all the long hours I worked each day, I still played competitive softball two or three nights a week during the summer and fall with my son Ty, and fished offshore nearly every Saturday with my son Terry.

Life is good, business is awesome, people are wonderful.

SIMPLE *fact*

> Your most valuable asset is your time. Maximize that time by creating new prospects every day.

Because I was intensely determined to make 40 to 70 sales each month, I quickly found out what would work—and what would not—when it came to finding new business and closing sales. I discovered what I've long called my *secret formula*: **CI + PPA = SOP**. I understood that if I first could get people to like me, I would close more sales. In turn, by combining my prospects liking me more than my competitors with the great products I had, plus really good service, plus a fair price for my products . . . I would win the sale more than 90% of the time.

One thing more: I can honestly tell you that, to this day, I have never tasted an alcoholic beverage, not even a beer. Oddly enough, years ago I did get pulled over by the police one night about 11:45 because the cops thought I was driving drunk. Back then I routinely used a little solar calculator. As I was driving home, I decided to figure out how much in commissions my four sales that day had earned. To power up my calculator, I held it up to the courtesy light in my car—while I kept driving. Evidently, I was weaving on the road when the police saw me. After being pulled over, the officers ordered me to get out of my car and actually do a sobriety test. I passed, of course, then explained what I had been doing. They laughed, but also suggested I wait until I got home to figure up my earnings for the day. A fine idea, I assured them.

The rest of my ride that night was downright exhilarating. There was nothing quite like the feeling of heading home from my last appointment at 11 p.m. with four or five sales under my belt for the day, and having calculated my commission in my head.

> One of the best things you can do for you family is to be successful at work. It's not a question of "either/or," but rather "both/and."

SIMPLE *fact*

"Hey, Ralph," I was telling myself, "when you walk in the door in a few minutes you can tell you family you made another $1,000 today!" That was one awesome feeling.

CHAPTER 13

The Fundamentals Will Not Let You Down

Authority follows those who take responsibility

POLICIES, PRODUCTS AND selling techniques often change, but the basic fundamentals of sales really don't. They've remained consistent for decades. James Samuel Knox wrote his classic *"Salesmanship"* in 1922—nearly a century ago. Napoleon Hill first published *"Think and Grow Rich"* in 1937, and Og Mandino's *"The Greatest Salesman in the World"* debuted in 1968. The fundamentals of sales that you'll find in those three best-sellers are every bit as relevant today as they were when they first appeared.

> Confused prospects will not buy. Worse, confused prospects won't ever admit to being confused.

SIMPLE *fact*

Although there are literally hundreds of sales-related fundamentals, I have identified 11 that I want to share. That's because they have helped me sell thousands of commercial and residential alarm systems and products.

1. **Keep it simple**—Do not overcomplicate the process.

   Chances are your prospects have never used the product you are trying to sell. Using industry jargon is likely to confuse your prospects. Confused prospects will not buy. Worse, confused prospects won't ever admit to being confused. When you do ask for the order, what you'll hear is, "I want to think it over"—just to get rid of you. Be sure to speak in a language that's simple and very easy to understand. It must appear to be very easy to purchase your product and use your product.

2. **Your self-image**—*As a security consultant, you should consider yourself as a life saver.*

One of the wonderful things I enjoy about this industry is the fact that what we do as sales people is not just protect property. We are also protecting lives. When you picture yourself as a life saver you will likely change the way you view every prospect you meet. Your attitude toward the safety of your prospects and their property will become obvious.

3. **Know your program**—*Knowledge overcomes fear.*

The more knowledge and information you have about your product, sales techniques, and your prospect, the better you will become at selling. Study everything you can get your hands on that relate to the various products you are selling. You should also subscribe to several of the free sales blogs on the internet. I personally subscribe to about 15 or more weekly publications. Selling security is what you do for a living. Why not become great at it?

SIMPLE *fact*

> There's a reason someone coined the phrase, "Timid sales people have skinny kids."

4. **Enthusiasm**—This is your belief in action.

Enthusiasm is one of the most important elements in a sales presentation. I could devote an entire chapter to the subject; that's how important enthusiasm is to all aspects of your sales career. Enthusiasm is contagious. It demonstrates confidence, and it's attractive. People naturally like being around excited, enthusiastic people. While sitting in the back row during one of my sales workshops, a young man once told me, *"Russ if I had your enthusiasm, I could make more sales."*

"You do have the enthusiasm," I instantly shot back. *"Just let it out!"*

Start acting more enthusiastic. Walk faster. Become more animated. Smile more. Fake it 'til you make it, as they say. There are 3 things you must be excited about:

Your product: You must believe you have the very best solution.

Your company: You must believe your company is the very best choice for your prospect.

Yourself: You must have within you the self-confidence to close every sale.

Remember: your prospect will never be more excited about your product than you are. You will make 100 times more sales by being enthusiastic than you will ever lose by being too enthusiastic. There's a reason someone coined the phrase, "Timid sales people have skinny kids."

5. **Control**—*Someone will control of your sales presentation; either you or your prospect.*

It had better be you. Always being control of your presentation is critical to the outcome of your sale. As you approach every sales opportunity, you'd better have a sound plan, too. While you have to expect interruptions during your presentation, you still should have an organized agenda of what you want to happen on each sales call.

I have been on plenty of calls when the prospect wanted to maintain control. There's no way I could let that happen. It's like a football team losing momentum at a critical point in a game. It's almost always doomed to defeat right then and there. The best way I've found to take control of a sales presentation is to simply ask questions.

One afternoon I had an appointment with a single woman of about 50, who had told me she wanted only "to discuss" protection for her home. She was an aeronautical engineer, and a very detailed individual. The first thing she told me as I entered was that she was "just shopping" for a security system and had no intention of buying, adding that she already had made appointments with other companies.

"And I don't need to see your sales pitch, either," my prospect stressed. "I just have a few questions."

"That will be fine, and I will more than happy to answer all your questions," I replied, all the while telling myself I *am* going to make this sale today.

Off she went reciting her list of questions. After the second one, I simply said, "Mary that was an interesting question. Do you mind me telling me why you asked it?" After she answered, my sales presentation was pretty much downhill from there. I was now in control.

I walked out of her home about an hour later with a spring in my step, a smile on my face . . . and a check in my top pocket. I have used that tactic countless times to gain or regain control of my sales presentation. So can you: Just ask questions.

6. **P.M.A.**—*Positive Mental Attitude*

You *must* believe that you can close every sales presentation. Develop a "no fear" attitude. Believe in yourself, and your ability to win the sale. If you ever do think you are not going to make the sale, you are correct. You won't.

SECURITY SYSTEMS SALES LEADERSHIP

So don't even waste your time trying. No matter what comes up—or even erupts—during your presentation, you need to have confidence that you can overcome any objection or situation.

7. **D.B.M.**—*Dominate Buying Motive*

You must have a clear understanding of this sales concept. As I mentioned in a previous chapter, my definition of a sale is to *find a need and fill it*. Before you can provide a solution for your prospect, you must know what the problem or need is. Alarm systems and surveillance systems are not a one-size-fits-all solution. A sales professional will first ask a series of questions before trying to determine the best solution for the prospect.

SIMPLE *fact* | One of the most interesting things that I have learned about people on sales calls is that they actually want you to relax and be comfortable.

8. **Act Normal**—*Be yourself*

I have endured way too many sales presentations where the consultant tried to appear to be more sophisticated that he or she actually was. There's no need for that. One of the most interesting things that I have learned about people on sales calls is that they actually want you to relax and be comfortable. This applies to both commercial and residential sales. You should always conduct yourself in a professional manner. But never try to impress anyone by acting like someone you are not.

9. **O.W.L.**—*Obsessed With Leads*

I consider myself to be always on duty. Whether I am at dinner with my family or at the boat ramp on Saturday launching my craft for a day on the water, I am always looking for that next prospect. Your business cards are your best prospecting tool. Have them with you at all times.

My wife and I own a second home in Steinhatchee, a town on the west coast of Florida that we visit most weekends. Its population is fewer than 1,000. If you drive along its streets, you won't have to look hard or long to find the yard signs and window stickers representing all the video and alarm systems I have sold there . . . during those weekend visits. Steinhatchee's Ace Hardware store, its two convenience stores, its bait shop and many residences are protected by the systems I sold. When I put my wallet in my pocket, my business cards go in next; every morning, seven days a week. Be obsessed with finding business.

10. **10. Urgency**—*Time kills deals*

   I am sure you can recall several situations when a possible sale never happened because someone did not move quickly enough. The fundamental of *urgency* is critical to your success. When you find prospects, don't hesitate to set appointments and get in front of them right away to deliver your dazzling sales presentation. What is important right now to a prospect might not be quite so important tomorrow. Whenever a prospect calls our office inquiring about our services, it is essential that we arrange an appointment ASAP. If a prospect calls in the morning, it's routine for me to have a sales consultant making a call a few hours later. *Strike while the iron is hot.*

   > Stay in control of your prospect by taking responsibility for the next move.

   SIMPLE *fact*

11. **Maintain responsibility for the relationship**—*Do not leave the responsibility for the next meeting or telephone call up to your prospect.*

   When I was the sales manager at Certified Security, I had a large, professionally designed sign installed for prominent display on the front wall of our sales room. The sign read: ***They don't call you back!***

   I grew oh so weary of my sales people telling me, "The prospect is going to call us back to let us know if she is going to buy or not." First of all, I was ticked off because we should have made the sale while we were in front of the prospect. And, now we're going to wait for the prospect to contact us to let us know they are ready to buy? "Not gonna happen!"

   Although I did sell over 90% of my presentations on the first call, I still had numerous business and residential prospects who did not buy immediately. Whenever a prospect would try to tell me, "I will call you back in a few days to let you know about our decision," I would politely explain, "I appreciate that, but it might be difficult for you to catch me on the telephone. So if it's OK with you, let me call you back at your convenience." My prospect would almost always agree, and I would then set a very specific day and time to call. Often, I would enter that information in my day planner as the prospect was watching.

   It is paramount that you assume responsibility for the sale. Stay in control of your prospect by taking responsibility for the next move.

   As in any sport, you must first learn and master the basic fundamentals, then build on those basics. Regardless of how experienced and skilled you may be, you can never forget the basic fundamentals. I never have. These fundamentals are what I lived by when I was in the field every day setting appointments and making sales. They also have helped me stay on the top of my game for decades.

There are no real short cuts for sales champions. So I urge you study what I have outlined in this chapter. They may seem fairly simple, or all too obvious. Perhaps. However, I have found that while many sales people understand them all, too many nevertheless fail to apply these simple fundamentals. And it's applying them that makes all the difference.

"Stick with the fundamentals. They will not fail you."

CHAPTER 14

Watch Your Language

YOU DON'T LOSE sales to other companies. You lose sales to a more professional sales person.

This may sound trivial. It's anything but. Too many sales people really do not understand the power of the words they utter when dealing with a prospective buyer. As a sales professional, your vocabulary will have a definite impact on your success. Yes, when conferring with your prospect, your body language and your non-verbal communication are extremely important, but not nearly as much as the words you use. What you say is a dead giveaway about your level of professionalism. Make every word matter.

> What you say is a dead giveaway about your level of professionalism. Make every word matter.

SIMPLE *fact*

Some words spoken by a sales person will instantly put fear in the mind of a prospect. By changing just a few words, I've found I can get my point across in a much softer and clearer, and more assuring way. So here is the list I've compiled of the negative verbiage, followed by the correct terms that my years in the alarm business tell me are far more acceptable to my prospects.

Negative: **Price** *or* **Cost**—Sounds too scary. No one likes the price of anything.

Positive: Invest—When your prospects invest in something, they feel like they are getting something in return and their money is being well spent.

Negative: Buy—Buy is always a negative word; avoid it.

SIMPLE *fact*

> Saying you are cheaper than the competition suggests your company and your product are both cheap.

Positive: Own—People like to own things, rather than buy things.

Negative: Contract—A terrible word that scares the daylights out of every buyer.

Positive: Agreement—Much more pleasant term because it indicates both parties are working together for a common cause.

Negative: Sign or Signature—Either of these words sounds too definite and firm, and can arouse doubts.

Positive: OK, Authorize, or **Autograph**—Using either of these terms makes it much easier for the prospect to give you the OK to go to work for them.

Negative: Deal—Using this term makes you sound too "slick".

Positive: Opportunity—Much more pleasant and easier and sounds much more positive.

Negative: Pitch—No one wants to see your sales pitch.

Positive: Presentation—This word sounds much more interesting and professional

Negative: Quote or Bid—This sounds unprofessional.

Positive: Proposal—Much more professional.

Negative: Customer—Old fashioned term for people who pay you money.

Positive: People We Serve—This term conveys that you are in a more subservient relationship with your new prospect; you are there to serve.

Negative: The System—Does not describe what it does.

Positive: The Protection—Describes the peace of mind your prospect is about to enjoy.

Negative: False Alarm—This term scares the heck out of your prospect. Never utter these two words in front of any prospect.

Positive: Accidental Alarm—Describes the event like it is no big deal. This is much more comfortable for you prospect.

Negative: Cheaper—Avoid using the word cheap unless you are referring to competitors. Saying you are cheaper than the competition suggests your company and your product are both cheap.

SIMPLE *fact*

Using the correct, positive terms not only will make you sound like a professional, but it also will separate you from the competition.

Positive: More Economical—We are not the low-cost provider. We are the low-risk provider.

Negative: Objection—Using this term in front of your prospect while discussing a decision not to buy sounds too final.

Positive: Area of Concern—This term makes an objection sound less like a road-block and more like a speed bump on your way to the sale.

Negative: Appointment—This word is for rookie sales people who are just getting started in their sales career. Appointments are usually thought of as negatives; such as a dentist appointment or an appointment with my lawyer.

Positive: Visit—Using this term will likely put your prospect at ease and sounds much more positive and pleasant.

Using the correct, positive terms not only will make you sound like a professional, but it also will separate you from the competition. There are just 13 sets of terms here for you to work on. Begin now to make the positives I've cited part of your daily vocabulary. It will be time and effort well spent.

CHAPTER 15

You Must Have a Pre-planned Presentation

Success is the result of relentless, proper action taken over time.

AFTER THREE DECADES, it still amazes me: So many sales people show up to do a presentation and have no organized plan for the meeting; none whatsoever. They expect to just "wing it" from start to finish by simply dealing with whatever comes up during the time they spend with their prospect. Most of these individuals are knowledgeable enough, and have a fine understanding of their product. But they still fail to maximize the opportunity right in front of them.

On every sales call I ever made there were four things I wanted to accomplish: first, of course, **make the sale**; second, **sell additional products and services**; third, sell **additional rate**; finally, get **referrals** from my new customer. I've always considered meeting with a new prospect to be an extraordinary opportunity. Whenever it comes along, I want to make sure I take my time and make the most of it.

I truly believe that if you represent a good company, and offer a good product at a fair price, you should win the sale most of the time. Even so, you will never really hit the home run with your new customer if you remain satisfied with just making the sale and moving on to the next prospect. As the adage goes, "Dance with the one you're with!" Sell the benefits and

> I really believe that if you represent a good company and offer a good product at a fair price you should win the sale most of the time.

SIMPLE *fact*

features of some of the cool products you have to offer and, by all means, *never ever* leave your new customer without first asking for referrals.

To really get the most from every presentation you make, you must have a plan before you ever step foot on your prospect's property. Wing it? Are you kidding!? You're wasting a precious opportunity. Seize your opportunities by following my nine-step preplanned presentation. What you're about to read has worked for me thousands of times, and it will work for you.

STEP 1: The pre-sale warm up

This might be the most important of all of the steps in any prepared presentation. This time is extremely important because you are about to build a relationship with your new prospect. Remember, *"People buy from individuals, not companies."* So do not rush these moments. Do your best to get your respective prospects to talk about themselves. If you can find something in common with your prospect, you will likely win the sale.

STEP 2: Fact finding

Just telling your prospect that you are the best or you provide the best service is not going to get the job done. Prove it!

As you have already read, one of my definitions of a sale is, *"Find a need and fill it."* If you don't understand what the true problem is, there is no way you can recommend a possible solution.

Can you imagine going to a doctor because you weren't feeling well and, without asking you what hurt or giving you some sort of check-up, your doctor wrote out a prescription? No physician has any reason for recommending a solution for any ailment without knowing what hurts. Sales is no different. You must examine your prospect's situation before you can recommend a solution. In turn, you must ask several questions and be very observant to determine the best *prescription* you can recommend to your prospect.

I always recommend preprinting a list of questions to ask your prospects. Having this "security questionnaire" delivers several benefits. First of all, it is a tool you can use to take control of your presentation. The questionnaire also helps generate conversation that will give you insights about a prospect's level of interest. And, this tool will give you an opportunity to introduce additional products and services your prospect might not be aware of. Finally, by going over this list of questions you will understand what the real need is, so you can provide the very best solution.

STEP 3: Sell your company

At this point in your presentation, you need to take a few minutes to talk about your company. How long have you been in business? What separates you from the competition? You should be able to provide documentation to affirm how you are better than the other guys. It is important during this step to provide a reason (other than price) on why your prospect should choose you to provide personal safety and protection for valuables. Just telling a prospect you are the best, or that you provide the best service, won't get get the job done. Prove it!

STEP 4: Demonstrate your product

This is where you can really separate yourself from your competitors, and dazzle your prospect with your exciting presentation. But you must have more than just a colorful brochure.

Impress your prospects by getting them *involved*. You would never buy a car or a home without checking it out in advance. The same goes for security systems. When I was actively selling every day, I always took a keypad with me to every presentation. I wanted to have my prospect actually touch the product. Although it was just a "dummy" keypad, it did the trick; I could illustrate how to arm and disarm the protection. Today my sales teams can fully demonstrate our products and capabilities with a live, working demo kit. If you are selling a video system, why not take along a few cameras to illustrate what you want your prospects to buy? If you are going to recommend interactive service as part of the protection, make sure you show them how the app works on a cell phone or tablet. This will help both eliminate any doubts that unfamiliarity can provoke and enhance a desire for you are selling.

STEP 5: The "Security Site Survey"

This step is especially significant: You not only are recommending specific locations where a prospect might need protection, but you also are reinforcing the fact that you are a security consultant and *the authority* when it comes protecting one's premises.

Here are a few guidelines to keep in mind as you conduct a security survey: 1) Whenever possible, make sure to have the **decision makers with you** as you walk the home or business. 2) **Never discuss price** during the survey; never! You are not ready to close this sales. Once you start quoting prices as you consider areas of protection, you will have to explain the costs, and this is not the place for doing that. 3) **Ask lots of questions**, and be prepared to offer recommendations and suggestions while you survey the property. 4) **Begin using possessive language**.

As you walking the home or business, refer to the protection your prospects might be considering as if they have already committed to purchasing the protection.

Say, for instance, I am in the kitchen of a home. During my site survey, I would say, *"Mr. and Mrs. Jones, this area here next to the door might be the perfect place for your keypad control. Wouldn't you agree with that?"*

Or, if I am dealing with an owner at his place of business, I might suggest, *"Mr. Jones, if you have a camera in this location in the warehouse, you will be able to observe everyone and everything that comes in and out of the back door. That makes sense, doesn't it?"*

SIMPLE *fact* | Perceived value must be higher than the investment.

One of your goals of any sales call is to sell additional products. A site survey well conducted will likely give you that opportunity. During my sales career, I sold thousands of dollars in additional products simply by asking my prospects how they felt about a particular product that might be a good fit for their home or business. A professionally done security site survey helped me close scores of additional sales. It will do the same for you.

STEP 6: Drive up perceived value

So now it's time to ask for the order, right? Not quite. First, be sure you have driven the perceived value to a level that's much higher than the investment. What does this mean? When you finally present the investment—i.e. ask for the order—your prospect must feel it really is a great deal. ***Perceived value* is what someone *thinks* something is worth.**

Sitting about 100 feet behind my home is my workshop. Since I live in Florida fairly close to the water, walking at night from my home's back door across the back yard to the workshop can be an frightening adventure. There's no telling what I'm liable to step on. We have seen opossums, raccoons, armadillos, and snakes—but, so far, at least no alligators. After enduring this challenge for a few weeks, I went to our local hardware store and purchased a motion- detector flood light and installed it over to door to my shop. That light is awesome! When I get within about 50 feet of my shop the light comes on and I can easily see my way to the door. I probably would have invested a good $200 or more in that light, because of value it delivers. Yet, its entire assembly, including the bulbs, cost me less than $50. To me, this was one great deal. The perceived value was much greater than the true cost.

You want your prospect feeling the same way about the protection you are presenting. Don't even allude to price until you have first driven up the perceived value well above the investment. And keep driving up perceived value all the way through your presentation. This all begins when you first meet your prospect. Mr. Jones or Ms. Smith initially must see value in *you*. You continue building value as you describe the benefits of your company. As you demonstrate your product, you are adding more value. As you point out features and benefits, you are adding even more value.

Always remember to **build value first**. The instant you quote price first, you put yourself in a position where you must justify your price. That's not where you want to be, so don't go there, not yet. When you finally do present the price, your prospect should be thinking, *"Wow, this is a great deal!"* As long the perceived value exceeds the price, it will be a great deal.

STEP 7: Ask for the order

I could include an entire chapter on this subject, but let's focus on the basics of what is always the most important step in any sales situation: closing the sale.

First of all, **always ask for the order.** No matter what—or even how emphatically—your prospect may have told you earlier in your presentation not to ask, ask for the order anyway! The No. 1 reason most sales people fail is that they *don't* ask for the order. If you don't ask, the answer is always . . . *no*.

When you ask, be sure to **use a tie-down question**. It's far different from an open-ended question. A tie-down question is one with an answer that can be written on your agreement. Here's an example: *"Mr. Jones, we can install your protection on Thursday or Friday. Which day is best?"* Read this question again. You are not asking *whether or not* your prospect is going to buy. You are assuming your prospect *is going* to buy.

Compare my recommended approach to an open-ended question, such as: *"Mr. Jones, do you want to go ahead and schedule an installation date for your protection?"* Ugh! This is a terrible question, because you now are asking for a Yes-or No-response. In truth, the only response you want is "Yes!" Change your question, and you will hear "Yes!" more often, and win more sales.

One caution: I never ask for the order until I am pretty sure I am going to hear "yes!" If I sense that my prospect is going to say "No," I won't ask for the order, not yet. Instead, I will continue asking questions, continue driving up perceived value, and continue selling.

So, how do you know when your prospect is likely to say "Yes!"? It's really pretty simple—if you know what to look for—and listen for—from your prospects: It's really a collection of what I call *buying signals* that your prospects will communicate with you. Here is a sample of buying signals, in no particular order:

1. They ask any questions about the installation of the protection.

2. They want to touch your demo, or pick up your brochure for the second time.

3. They demonstrate an evident change in body language that suggests more intent interest.

4. They ask detailed questions about the use of the protection.

5. They ask questions about options that might come with the product.

6. They ask questions about price or payment plans.

7. They begin using possessive language.

Another technique I always use when closing the sale is the *alternative-of-choice* close. Instead of presenting my price and asking for the order, I typically give my prospect three choices of protection levels they should consider: Plan A . . . Plan B or Plan C.

For any sales representative, this is a moment of truth, the time when you muster the most confidence and enthusiasm you have. As you take this step in your presentation, you are about to find out how just good a job you have done thus far.

SIMPLE *fact* | "Referrals are the life blood of your sales career."

As I present these plans to my prospect, my conversation goes something like this: *"Mr. Jones, I have created three different levels of protection for your business. Now, please understand I am not necessarily recommending any one of these plans over the others. You need to choose the one that is most comfortable for you, and will give you the piece of mine you are looking for."*

After making that brief introduction of my three plans, I will go into great detail explaining each item listed in each plan, and quote the *investment* of each one. (notice both the word I used and the one I avoided). As I conclude this explanation, I then ask this question: *"Mr. Jones, if you were to make a buying decision right now for the protection and peace of mind for your property, which plan is best for you?"*

Once you ask for the order . . . Shut up! Wait for the answer. You may well be tempted to keep talking. Avoid that temptation. Wait for your prospect to respond.

STEP 8: Ask for referrals

After your prospect has committed to buy, you will be tempted to pack up and leave. Hang in there. You have one more important step to deal with that will make you a boat load of money.

Referrals are the life blood of your sales career. If you can master how to pull referrals from every customer you sell, you will be overwhelmed with leads, so much so that won't ever have to hit the streets to find new business. And you won't have the time to begin with. You will accumulate hundreds of prospects in a very short time if you simply slow down and ask for referrals.

The myriad nuances and techniques for pulling referrals is beyond the scope of these pages. For now, focus on what for me has been an obsession: Getting referrals along the sale. I believe firmly that I should be able to get at least 10 to 20 names of friends and family members from everyone I sold to. Consider this example, extreme as it is:

I once had an appointment with a retired judge, in his office. He sounded like a challenge. Before our meeting, I had learned that the judge was a collector of law books, did not have much of a personality, and was not well liked by his peers. Ominous as all that sounded, I still was determined not only to get the sale, but that I also would sell the judge additional products *and* get a bunch of referrals. As I closed my presentation—and after I had gotten his commitment to buy additional protection—I simply asked the judge for the names and telephone numbers of about 100 attorneys in town that he knew (I wasn't kidding about this being an extreme example). I had never asked anyone for 100 referrals before, and certainly never at a business.

To my surprise, the judge called his assistant into the office. He then told her to take me into the library . . . and give me the names of all the lawyers in town he had done business with! His directive blew me away. After I departed, I remember how I started counting names and numbers. I had amassed a list of 70. I also well remember making my first sale from that list later that afternoon.

People often ask me how I averaged between 50 and 80 sales per month selling commercial and residential alarms. My response is simple: "I pull massive numbers of referrals from every customer I meet." For me, pulling referrals always has been as important as closing the sale, and acting on my own advice: "*"If you don't ask, the answer is always no."*

STEP 9: The "tie down"

This final step in your sales presentation is the briefest. But it's also important. This is the time you sincerely thank your new customer for trusting you to provide the protection just purchased. Remind your customer what's to happen next. Perhaps Mr. Jones or Ms. Smith will receive a telephone call from your office, reminding them of the date and time the protection will be installed.

You should also hand your new customer several of your business cards, and ask they be passed along to friends or colleagues might have an interest in doing business with you.

And, if you really want to make a great impression on your new customer, do what a true overachiever will do: Sometime within an hour or so after your presentation and sale, make a brief "selfie" video and text it to your new customer as a thank you. You'll be surprised at the impression you will leave with your new customer.

And you'll be that much closer to your next sale.

One Last Thing:
Sell With Integrity

*"Life is not important except in the impact
it has on other lives."*—Jackie Robinson

I CANNOT REMEMBER precisely when it all began, only that it was a Monday morning, around 9 or so. While reviewing my day planner and preparing to hit the road and sell some more alarm systems, my phone rang.

"I'm transferring you a call," our receptionist said matter-of-factly. In a few seconds, I was listening to a Mrs. Dottie Varnell. I had sold a security system to one of her friends from her church, she explained, and she wanted me to come see her.

"I'll be happy to drop by this morning," I replied quickly. "My calendar's open, and I can be at your home in an hour." That would be fine, Mrs. Varnell said in a pleasant voice. Before long I was off.

She lived in a very nice neighborhood of beautiful homes. Immediately after responding to my knock and saying hello, she started reminding me how her friend had recommended me. I was a man whom she could trust to take care of her security needs, Mrs. Varnell's friend had told her. Naturally, I expressed my gratitude and promised to do my best to live up to such an introduction.

As we stood in the foyer of her home, Mrs. Varnell went on to say that her husband had passed away about a month earlier.

"I'm now alone for the first time," she allowed, "and frankly it's frightening." In addition, she had a medical condition that further concerned her. So she wanted "total protection" for both her home and herself. Money was "no problem," she added pointedly.

"Be very careful when you tell a sales person money is not going to be a problem," I advised, only partly in jest. "Some sales people will see dollar signs as an opportunity take advantage of you."

With that, I began my usual site survey of her home. Once I finished, I began pricing the various levels of protection I was going to offer. But in the midst of explaining the three options that I had prepared for her, Mrs. Varnell gently took my price sheet from my hand, and began asking what *additional* protection I could offer. Her gesture was a bit surprising, but I kept explaining, outlining the value of glass-break sensors at certain places in her home, plus locations for a few medical panic buttons.

It was now apparent that I really didn't have to do much selling. My new customer wanted to add a glass-break detector in *every* room in her home, including the bathrooms and her garage! The option she was most interested in was loaded with . . . motion detectors . . . glass-break sensors . . . two sirens . . . three key pads . . . medical buttons in every room . . . a wireless key fob, and fire protection. All told, Mrs. Varnell was about to invest more than $3,600 in a security system for a home of less than 2,000 square feet.

Make no mistake. I believe firmly that when it comes to buying protection for a home or a business, customers should invest in whatever it takes to both give them sufficient protection and provide them with ample piece of mind. Even so, this was overkill, pure and simple. Mrs. Varnell was making a very emotional decision, and I needed to honor her trust in me—not abuse it.

"Mrs. Varnell, I've got tell you this," I began. "If you were my mother, I would not recommend spending $3,600 for the security that you are considering. We can provide you with more than adequate protection for a package that will cost about $2,100."

"Really?" she asked. "Well, OK," she quickly agreed, thanking me for my candor and honesty. "As long as you're sure."

I was sure, I affirmed her. Besides, I pointed out, once the protection I was recommending was installed, she could always add more later on if she still was not comfortable. After signing the necessary papers and arranging for the installation, I did what I what I always do: I asked Mrs. Varnell for referrals. She was more than happy to provide some, along with her most sincere thank you.

You can imagine the special feeling of satisfaction I had as I got back behind the wheel and headed for my next appointment. Moments later, though, my pager alerted me—which tells you how long it's been since Mrs. Varnell and I first met. The number that appeared was one I didn't recognize. So I pulled off the road and dialed it. It was Mrs. Varnell's son, calling from his downtown Jacksonville office at CSX Transportation. Oh, dear, I feared. Here comes a complaint about my sale to his mom. But what I heard was just the opposite: He was *thanking* me for treating her with respect, and saving her about $1,500.

"You're saving me some of my inheritance," Don Varnell even joked.

As we spoke, I figured I'd strike while the iron was hot. I told him his mother had given me his name and number as a referral, and that I had planned to call him to inquire about protecting his home.

"To tell you the truth, I really don't want a security system," he said, "but I'm still going to buy one from you because of what you've done for mom."

That same Monday afternoon I went to Don Varnell's home and sold a second security system . . . and then asked Don for referrals. He, too, gave me several, the very last one being his church, Terry Parker Baptist Church. It came with a key disclosure: in just two days, church officials would sign a contract with ADT for a system to protect their three buildings.

"I'd like you to go to the church, survey the buildings, and send me your proposal," Varnell said. He was chairman of the deacon board, he explained, and his board members would likely go along with whatever he recommended.

I beat a path to the church door the next morning. Before noon I had faxed my security survey and proposal of the buildings to my new friend, Don Varnell. Don called back by mid-afternoon to tell me he would recommend my company (Scott Alarm) for the job. Be at the pastor's office on Wednesday evening at 6 for the deacons meeting, he instructed, and be prepared to make my presentation to his board.

Don Varnell was as good as his word. After introducing me to the committee members, he proceeded to tell the story of what I had done for his mother 48 hours earlier. Yes, my price was slightly higher than ADT's price, he noted, but he still was going to recommend my proposal. The vote to hire Scott Alarm to protect Terry Parker Baptist Church was unanimous.

That sale was one of the largest I had ever made. The church invested thousands of dollars in protection. I even wound up selling security systems to several of its staff members . . . and all because I had treated Dottie Varnell like I would want a sales rep to treat my own mother.

But my saga doesn't end here.

Scott Alarm grew significantly. We opened offices in every major city in the Southeast. But I was rarely in any of them; I was on the go constantly. But I was at my desk one day when, once again, our receptionist transferred me a call.

"Mr. Ackerman, good morning. It's Don Varnell," he said cheerfully. Crazy as it sounds I could not recall his name until he mentioned Terry Parker Baptist Church.

My momentary amnesia didn't bother Don one bit, and he quickly began telling me he now was in a new home that needed an alarm system. Flattered though I was, I had to explain how I much I was traveling and that it kept me from doing outside sales.

"Let me recommend one of my best colleagues. He'll take extra good care of you," I replied.

"No, I want you," Varnell insisted. "If you can't come yourself, frankly I'd rather call ADT."

"When can we get together?" I asked quickly. As I jotted down the information for the appointment, his new address struck a chord. Don Varnell was now living in an upscale neighborhood. It aroused my curiosity, which then produced a revelation:

"I won the state lottery," Varnell acknowledged, trying to sound ho-hum about it.

Two days later, we met at his new home, one that was every bit as beautiful as I had expected. After completing the security survey, Don Varnell invested just over $3,600 in security protection—the very same amount his mother Dottie had originally wanted to invest a few years earlier. Much more than a co-incidence? I wonder.

This story—as true as can be—will forever remain one of my favorites, because of the three lessons it offers: 1) *Always* ask for referrals. 2) Sell from your heart, not your pocket book. 3) Treat every prospect like you would want your family member treated.

"If you help enough people get out of life what they want, you will have everything in your life that you want."—Zig Ziglar

Turn Your Sales Into Sensations With Contests

"Success is waking up in the morning and bounding out of bed because there's something out there that you love to do, that you believe in, that you're good at." —Whit Hobbs

THIS BOOK WOULD not be complete if I didn't share seven of the hottest, most successful sales contests I have used just within the past few years. It would be like delivering a great presentation but not asking for the order. Each of these contests were successful. Some were very short sprints; three lasted for approximately a month. So, let your creative juices flow and turn your sales into sensations with contests.

It's worth repeating: if you are going to run a contest, make a big deal out of it. For example, we *always* decorated the office to help everyone in the branch catch the excitement. On occasion, our sales manager even wore a costume to further stoke enthusiasm. And don't be afraid to get a little crazy and have fun. You're more than welcome to use any or all of these ideas—or adapt them as you see fit. So get excited, have some fun, and watch your sales increase. I can almost assure you they will.

Scavenger Hunt

January 5-18

The one remains my all-time favorite contest, and one I've conducted several times. Our first-ever Hunt started first thing on a Monday, at our 9 a.m. sales meeting. When team members began arriving about 8:45, they found the sales room decorated like a jungle, from floor to ceiling. Plants and vines and large pictures of animals were everywhere, while the sounds of jungle music drifted down from the room's loudspeaker, just loud enough to be heard. I also changed everyone's names on the sales board to reflect our contest: B'wana Bobby . . . Slayer Steve . . . Hank the Hunter . . . Jungle Jim . . . you get the idea. And as we began I issued each team member a safari hat that was to be worn during each morning's meeting.

We had a blast each and every day as team members came in and reported what they had "bagged" from the preceding day's hunt. Here are the details:

Contest objective: Earn 300 points and enjoy a full day of deep sea fishing on January 26.

Contest rules (*"Big Game" targets and point values*):

- Make 10 sales: 20 points
- Sell 1 extra keypad: 10
- Sell 1 extra motion detector: 10
- Make 2 approved sales in one day: 10
- Get 20 referrals from a customer: 10
- Sell $300 in add-ons to one customer: 10
- Set and sell a self-gen. in the same day: 10
- Self-gen. sale (unlimited): 10 per
- Set 2 self-gens. in one day: 10
- Turn in 30 business cards: 10
- Sell $200 in add-ons to one customer: 5
- Sell someone who lives on a numbered street: 5
- Get 10 referrals from a customer: 5
- Sell 1 smoke detector: 5
- Sell 1 strobe light: 5
- Takeover a First Alert system: 5

- Get the customer to set an appointment for you: 5
- Sell someone with an even-numbered zip code: 5
- Sell someone with 7 or more letters in their last name: 10
- Have your customer talk to Russ and tell him how attractive you are: 10

Daily prizes may be won by completing the daily hunt: Each day you will draw for some special activity that you must complete. By completing your daily activity you will have a chance to bag the prize that is behind the photo of the animal you shoot in the meeting room. Daily prizes and daily activity will vary and likely will be different from day to day.

The *Scavenger Hunt* always generated loads of enthusiasm for our sales teams. Most important, each time I have conducted it sales have increased. In fact, the first time I conducted this contest, *everyone* hit his or her numbers.

April Month-End
Monday—Thursday

Contest rules:

• Door and window contacts: "Buy one, get one free"

• Motion Detectors: $59

• 6 approved self-gen sales before the Friday sales meeting (May 1) and win $500 cash bonus

• All self-generated sales must be *new* prospects, not people you have demo-ed before, or appointments you set during a home show.

• Self gens may be prospects that you walk up, referrals that you set on your own, calls you make from the leads you got from the home show or anyone that calls in from your activity.

• All self-gen sales must be made during this period and must be approved by 9 a.m. Tuesday (May 5).

April Showers Brings May Flowers
Bonuses!! Self-generated sales and unit bonus for the month

Contest rules:

• 3 Self-Generated Sales: $75

• 6 Self-Generated Sales: $200

• 10 Self-Generated Sales: $500

There will be an additional $50 bonus paid for every self-generated sale beginning with the 11th sale, with no cap.

In addition to the self-generated bonuses, there will be a $500 unit bonus paid once 20 approved sales are turned in. To qualify for the unit bonus, you must have a minimum of 10 self- generated sales.

Friends & Family
August 19—September 16 @ 9 a.m.

Contest rules:

• This is a referral sales contest. Only sales made from a referral list dated during the contest period can be counted.

• All appointments must be set by the **consultant or the referring customer**. Referral appointments set by the company will not count for this contest.

• If a referral already on the list of referrals calls in, it will be counted toward contest rewards.

• All referrals must come from a customer.

• Sales consultants may go back to existing customers for referrals, but they must be turned in on a referral form dated during the contest to be counted for contest rewards.

• Referrals must be turned in *each day* during the sales meeting. The managers will then fax or email the referrals to Russ immediately after the sales meeting concludes.

• There will be a simple spread sheet with all the referrals listed from each sales person, so everyone can view and track results. This referral list will be sent out each day to the entire sale team.

• A consultant may not count any referrals they received before the contest began.

• Only approved sales will count.

• Here is what consultants can win:

2 referral sales: *"Sort of friendly"* $50 Publix Gift Card.

5 referral sales: *"Very friendly"* Tom Hopkins's Series on *"How to Master the Art of Selling Anything"* (this is really awesome).

8 referral sales: *"Great Social Skills"* $300 Amex/Visa Gift Card.

12 referral sales: *"Charismatic"* Weekend at Sea World, including 2 park passes and $200 in spending money.

15 referral sales: *"Customers Love You"*—4-day Carnival Cruise for 2 from Port Canaveral.

March Madness 2014

Dates: March 10—April 6

Contest rules:

• The sales manager will be the coach.

• On Monday March 10, each sales room will be decorated with a basketball theme.

• Each sales rep has been given a "basketball" related name; example: "Magic Mike".

• Points will be scored as follows:

Self-gen sale = **2 points.**

Self-gen sale with either $300 in add-ons, 10 referrals, or $45 rate = **3 points.**

Company provided lead = **1 point (free throw).**

Company provided lead with either $300 in add-ons, 10 referrals, or $45 in rate = **2 points**

The Score Board and Awards:

6 points = $25 36 points = $250

12 points = $50 42 points = $300

18 points = $100 48 points = $350

24 points = $150 54 points = $400

30 points = $200 60 points = $450

Bonus dollars are accumulative; for example, a player scoring 42 points would earn a total of $1075 in basketball bucks.

• The sales manager will update the score board throughout the day.

• Each day in the sales meeting, the coach will reward the players on his team with basketball bucks that they earned the previous day.

• All referrals that are counted for points must be turned in during the sales meeting to the coach or they cannot be counted.

• *Contest within the contest:* We will set up a nerf type basketball goal set in the sales room for reps to shoot free throws each day. The sales manager may determine who qualifies to shoot free throws for company leads each day.

March Madness

March 26—April 2 (one full week)

"We are having a great month for the district, but haven't yet won the championship. We are pushing the ball up the floor, with enough time left on the clock to set up a wide-open, game-winning shot. So let's move, score, and win! Every sales consultant needs to get motivated *this month* to help make it happen. We can do it!"

Contest rules:

• All sales must be in the booking system with the appropriate date of sale.

• The attached tracking form must be submitted for approval by April 4.

• Each sales consultant will receive a copy of the tracking form.

• All sales must be dated during the contest term (March 26—April 1)

• Any sale generated during the contest and needs to be have paperwork "cleaned up", such as a credit cosigner or other paperwork issues must be complete by Tuesday morning April 3rd. at 9:00 AM

• All money won during this contest will be added to regular payroll:

5 approved sales: $100 — 7 approved sales: $150 — 10 approved sales: $250

March Madness Tracking Form

Sales Consultant: _____

(List each sale and date)

1. _____ Date: _____ Admin OK

2. _____ Date: _____ Admin OK

3. _____ Date: _____ Admin OK

4. _____ Date: _____ Admin OK

5. _____ Date: _____ Admin OK

6. _____ Date: _____ Admin OK

7. _____ Date: _____ Admin OK

8. _____ Date: _____ Admin OK

9. _____ Date: _____ Admin OK

10. _____ Date: _____ Admin OK

_____

Sales Manager/Branch Manager Signature

My Heart's In It

February 1 - 28

Goal: Create energy, excitement and team unity in each branch while driving up sales, rate, add-ons and referrals. *"Let's get back to having fun with sales."*

Contest Guidelines:

• Each **self-generated** sale will earn you **1 heart**.

• Each time you turn in **10 referrals** from one sale you earn **1 heart**.

• Each sale that has a rate of **$49.95** or more will earn you **1 heart**.

• Each sale that includes **$200** or more in additional protection will earn you **1 heart**.

Example: If Mike sells a **self-gen** and gets $39.95 in rate, but also gets **10 referrals** and **$250 in add-ons** he would earn **3 hearts** for that one sale.

Here is how and what you can win:

• **20 Hearts:** a $150 gift card to **Ruth's Chris Steak** House for you and your best friend.

• **18 Hearts:** a $75 gift card to **Outback Steakhouse** for you and your best friend.

• **16 Hearts:** a $50 gift card to **Longhorn Steakhouse** for you and your best friend.

• **14 Hearts:** a $15 gift card to **Subway** for you and your best friend.

Everyone Can Win!

Note:

• All hearts will be counted at the end of the contest. A consultant can only win one gift card.

• A copy of all referrals to be counted in the contest must be turned into the sales manager.

• Sales managers will be responsible for decorating their sales rooms with lots of bright hearts on the walls and hanging from the ceiling.

• Sales managers must also create a score board to track each sales consultant and place the hearts earned beside the correct names.

Self-Gen Contest

February 22—28

Contest rules:

• Only self-gen sales that you set *on your own* will count. Anyone who calls in the office for you will not be considered a self-gen for this contest.

• Only self-gen appointments set during the contest period may be counted (example: appointments set before Monday, Feb. 22, will not count).

• All bonus money earned will be added to your commission.

Here is what you can win:

1st Self-gen approved sale: $20 Bonus

2nd Self-gen approved sale: $40 Bonus

3rd Self-gen approved sale: $80 Bonus

4th Self-gen approved sale: $160 Bonus

5th Self-gen approved sale: $320 Bonus

About the Author

RUSS ACKERMAN IS the President of Proven Sales Strategies, a company that does consulting for alarm companies and holds seminars to train sales leaders and sales consultants in the alarm industry. He is also holds the current position of director of Residential and Small Business Sales for Atlantic Security in Jacksonville, Florida. Russ started his career, in the alarm business, in 1986 with Scott Alarm, in Jacksonville Florida. Between the years of 1986 and 1991 he personally sold over 3500 residential and small business alarm systems.

Russ has been awarded a variety of industry awards including the prestigious Honeywell Medal of Honor. He is a noted speaker at various seminars and training programs throughout the country. Throughout his career he has trained hundreds of successful sales consultants and managers.

Russ is also a contributing editor for Security Sales and Integration Magazine and writes security related articles for area newspapers. When he is not training, Russ enjoys offshore fishing and is a U.S. Coast Guard Licensed Charter Boat Captain.

Do you want to become a
BETTER SALES LEADER?

Are you seeking ways to
MAKE MORE SALES?

Register now to get
FREE WEEKLY SALES TIPS.

Apply for the
PROVEN SALES STRATEGIES
VIP Program!

We'll meet with you FACE-TO-FACE
at
YOUR OFFICE!

CONTACT US TODAY AT:

rackerman@provensalesstrategies.com

or visit us on the web at:

www.provensalesstrategies.com

Made in the USA
Columbia, SC
16 January 2023

10254155R00074